Moral Infringement and Repair in Antiquity

Supplement 1: *Emotions and Hierarchies*

Studia Theologica Holmiensia 35

Thomas Kazen

Moral Infringement and Repair in Antiquity

Supplement 1:

Emotions and Hierarchies

Enskilda Högskolan Stockholm
2022

ISBN: 978-91-88906-18-2

Cover design: Carl Johan Berglund.
Cover images: Fragments of Roman wall painting (first century CE).
Metropolitan Museum of Art. Public domain.
Typeset in EB Garamond.
Printed by BoD – Books on Demand, Norderstedt, Germany.

Enskilda Högskolan Stockholm
Åkeshovsvägen 29, 168 39 Bromma
www.ehs.se

Preface

The present volume presents results from the project "Dynamics of Moral Repair in Antiquity," funded by the Swedish Research Council, grant nr. 2016-02319, between 2017 and 2021. The main publication, *Interpersonal Infringement and Moral Repair: Revenge, Compensation and Forgiveness in the Ancient World* is forthcoming in 2023 with Mohr Siebeck, in the WUNT series.

However, during the course of the project we have also produced a number of journal articles and book chapters. Most of these are now being collected and republished by EHS (Enskilda Högskolan Stockholm = University College Stockholm) in a number of supplementary volumes, which will be available both in print and freely online (ehs.se/moralrepair).

Supplement 1: *Emotions and Hierarchies*, contains four articles and chapters by Thomas Kazen. Three of them are republished in accordance with the publishers' general conditions for author reuse. The fourth has not been published before. Only minor corrections have been made. The sources are as follows:

"Emotional Ethics in Biblical Texts: Cultural Construction and Biological Bases of Morality," *Hebrew Bible and Ancient Israel* 6 (2017): 434–459

"Viewing Oneself through Others' Eyes: Shame between Biology and Culture in Biblical Texts," *Svensk Exegetisk Årsbok* 84 (2019): 51–80.

"Law and Emotion in Moral Repair: Circumscribing Infringement," *Journal for the Study of the Old Testament* 46.4 (2021): 545–560.

Stockholm School of Theology, Bromma, June 2022

Thomas Kazen & Rikard Roitto

Contents

Emotional Ethics in Biblical Texts

Cultural Construction and Biological Bases of Morality

Abstract

In the evolution of human beings as a successful social species, emotions have played a crucial role. This article focuses on the role of empathy for moral discernment, and especially on its role for an expanding altruism. Although a cultural construct, morality rests on emotional underpinnings which have ensured the survival of humankind. Some of these mechanisms are illustrated by a discussion of select biblical and Second Temple period Jewish texts, including texts from the Covenant Code, Deuteronomy, the Holiness Code, Proverbs, Genesis, and ben Sira. Special attention is given to definitions of altruism, the role of kin, and potentials for expanding empathy beyond assumed limits.

Introduction

This article explores a selection of texts from the Hebrew Bible in order to illustrate the role of biologically based emotions for moral discernment. The differing and sometimes conflicting ethics, not only between cultures, but also within one and the same culture, that are attested by these ancient texts, certainly indicate that morality is a social and cultural construct, which develops and changes over time. At the same time, certain emotional underpinnings for human morality, which have evolved as intrinsic traits through evolutionary adaptation for the survival of humanity as a social species, are also clearly visible through biblical texts. This fits with the understanding that moral norms are formed and transformed through a continuous interactive process, governed by biologically based and culturally construed reactions and behaviours, combined in an inseparable blend. This process becomes particularly visible in the study of altruistic and prosocial ideals and norms, and the ways in which these are developed, negotiated, and implemented in various texts and contexts. I will thus focus on examples of empathy and altruism in arguing my case.

Theory

Moral Emotions and Moral Foundations

During the last few decades there has been an interesting move away from an un-derstanding of morality as primarily based on rational deliberations (as in Law-rence Kohlberg's type of developmental psychology),[1] to a more complex under-standing of how moral choices and moral behaviours are based on a complex in-teraction between intuition and rationality, in which emotions play a (if not *the*) crucial role.[2] A number of factors have contributed to this development, especially within the fields of evolutionary biology, evolutionary psychology,[3] and neurosci-ence.[4]

One of the early landmarks was Antonio Damasio's book *Descartes' Error*, which, based on neurobiological research, demonstrated how rational thinking ends up in dysfunctional action when emotions are impaired. Emotion and intui-tion (which is an emotional function) are simply integral parts of human cognition and decision-making.[5] Other important evidence came from psychological exper-iments, such the "trolley problem" experiments by Joshua Greene and colleagues;[6] the experiments of Jorge Moll and colleagues, comparing the degree of emotional

---

[1] Cf. Lawrence Kohlberg, *The Philosophy of Moral Development: Moral Stages and the Idea of Justice* (San Francisco: Harper & Row, 1981); Lawrence Kohlberg *et al.*, *Moral Stages: A Cur-rent Formulation and a Response to Critics* (Contributions to Moral Development 10; Basel: Karger, 1983).

[2] Jonathan Haidt, "The Emotional Dog and Its Rational Tail: A Social Intuitionist Ap-proach to Moral Judgment," *Psychological Review* 108 (2001): 814–834; idem, "The Moral Emo-tions," in *Handbook of Affective Sciences* (ed. Richard J. Davidson, Klaus R. Scherer, and H Hill Goldsmith; Oxford: Oxford University Press, 2003); idem, *The Righteous Mind: Why Good Peo-ple Are Divided by Politics and Religion* (London: Allen Lane, 2012); Joshua D. Greene, *Moral Tribes: Emotion, Reason, and the Gap between Us and Them* (New York: Penguin Press, 2013). Note that this evaluation of the role of emotion for morality neither places emotion in opposition to cognition (but rather regards it as part of cognition), nor implies that moral decisions ought to comply with emotional reactions.

[3] Taking over from the much (and often unjustly) discredited sociobiology; cf. Haidt, *Right-eous Mind*, 33–36.

[4] Haidt provides an account of this development (with an autobiographical touch) within the overall argument of *Righteous Mind*; cf. Greene, *Moral Tribes*.

[5] Antonio Damasio, *Descartes' Error: Emotion, Reason and the Human Brain* (New York: Grosset, 1996).

[6] See for example Joshua D. Greene *et al.*, "An fMRI Investigation of Emotional Engage-ment in Moral Judgment," *Science* 293 (2001): 2105–2108; idem, *Moral Tribes*.

involvement in different types of judgments;[7] Jonathan Haidt's experiments on how moral decisions relate to rational motivation, resulting in a "social intuitionist model";[8] and experiments on animal "proto-morality" by Frans de Waal and others.[9] All of these suggest that much Western thinking has been mistaken, based as it is on a dichotomous anthropology, from Plato's and Aristotle's ideals that reason should be the master over the passions,[10] to Immanuel Kant's categorical imperative.[11] Recent research on moral decision-making has clearly come out in favour of David Hume's view that reason is subordinate to the emotions.[12] And from an evolutionary perspective, this is why human rationality evolved in the first place. John Teehan expresses it well:

> We are emotional beings whose strivings for well-being, in a highly complex social environment, is enhanced by the means of reason. Reason does not have its own kind of contentment, if by that is meant a nonemotional one.[13] ... From an evolutionary perspective we must see reason and emotion as physiologically related functions of a highly complex organism – evolutionary strategies with the same end.[14]

---

[7] Jorge Moll *et al.*, "The Neural Basis of Human Moral Cognition," *Nature Reviews: Neuroscience* 6 (2005): 799–809.

[8] Haidt, "Emotional Dog."

[9] The literature is vast. For a few examples, see Frans de Waal, *Good Natured: The Origins of Right and Wrong in Humans and Other Animals* (Cambridge, MA: Harvard University Press, 1996); Stephanie D. Preston and Frans de Waal, "Empathy: Its Ultimate and Proximate Bases," *Behavioural and Brain Sciences* 25 (2002): 1–72; Frans de Waal, *Primates and Philosophers: How Morality Evolved* (The University Center for Human Values Series; Princeton, NJ: Princeton University Press, 2006); Sarah F. Brosnan, "'Nonhuman Species' Reactions to Inequity and their Implications for Fairness," *Social Justice Research* 19 (2006): 153–185; Marc Bekoff and Jessica Pierce, *Wild Justice: The Moral Lives of Animals* (Chicago, IL: University of Chicago Press, 2009).

[10] Cf. Simo Knuuttila and Juha Sihvola, "How the Philosophical Analysis of Emotions was Introduced," in *The Emotions in Hellenistic Philosophy* (ed. Juha Sihvola and Troels Engberg-Pedersen; The New Synthese Historical Library 46; Dordrecht: Kluwer Academic Publishers, 1998), 1–19.

[11] Cf. John Teehan, "Kantian Ethics: After Darwin," *Zygon* 38 (2003): 49–60.

[12] In contrast to Kant, for whom reason was seen as having no function to preserve the human organism, but only to produce human morality, Hume regarded emotions as primary and reason as secondary, in the sense that reason actually serves the emotions and is subordinate to them.

[13] I.e., reason cannot gain a satisfaction which is non-emotional; hence reason cannot really "drive" development or overrule emotion because there is emotional satisfaction (contentment) involved even in following reason.

[14] Teehan, "Kantian Ethics," 54.

Against the background of the overwhelming evidence for the role emotions play in human morality,[15] Jonathan Haidt has sorted emotions into families. Other-condemning emotions, including contempt, anger, and disgust, guard the moral order. Self-conscious emotions, including shame, embarrassment, guilt, and pride, constrain individual behaviour in a social context. Other-suffering emotions, including empathy, induce altruism and prosocial action. Other-praising emotions, including awe, elevation, and gratitude, respond to good deeds.[16] Based on Gewirth's understanding of morality, Haidt also construed a taxonomy of moral emotions, understood as "emotions that are linked to the interests or welfare either of society as a whole or at least of persons other than the judge or agent."[17] Based on this definition, emotions were ranked, so that those triggered by disinterested elicitors[18] and motivating prosocial actions were considered more moral than others. As a result, empathy scored high, fear scored low, and disgust came somewhere in between.[19] The taxonomy was admittedly speculative and rested on a definition of morality as mainly an interest in welfare. With different definitions, more emotions can be understood as crucial for morality.

This is precisely what is implied by Haidt's more recent publications on "moral foundations theory," which suggest six evolved universal cognitive modules (or "taste receptors") that are correlated to various emotions and form the basis for cultural constructions of morality: care/harm, fairness/cheating, loyalty/betrayal, authority/subversion, sanctity/degradation, and finally, liberty/oppression.[20] Although it is possible to argue that in some way, welfare (and hence empathy) is in-

---

[15] There is no room for details here. For further discussion of some of the evidence mentioned, see Thomas Kazen, *Emotions in Biblical Law: A Cognitive Science Approach* (Sheffield: Sheffield Phoenix, 2011), and for extensive reviews and references, see Haidt, *Righteous Mind*; and Greene, *Moral Tribes*.

[16] Haidt, "Moral Emotions."

[17] Haidt, "Moral Emotions," 853 (original italics removed).

[18] I.e., they are not the immediate result of one's own needs or interests.

[19] Depending on the extent to which these emotions are understood to be related to one's own interests or the welfare of others.

[20] Haidt, *Righteous Mind*, 112–186. The last moral foundation, "liberty/oppression," Haidt added relatively recently, after realizing that the five initial foundations did not capture "conservative notions of fairness, which focused on proportionality, not equality" (169). It should be pointed out that although Haidt's "moral foundations theory" draws in part on cross-cultural anthropological and psychological research, it is construed with a view to the present political landscape in the United States and is employed in order to understand and explain the conflicting values of Democrats and Republicans in particular. The model is open to criticism from a variety of angles; for a critical view from within the same American cultural and political sphere, see Greene, *Moral Tribes*, 334–346.

volved in all six, this requires a broadened view of welfare, and as a result neither fear, nor disgust, would necessarily be less important in the construction of morality than empathy is. Moreover, we need to understand morality in a broader sense than is common in the Western world, which usually regards it from an individualistic perspective, separate from social conventions and community concerns.[21]

Disgust, for example, is involved in evaluations of a range of behaviours and conditions, from taboos and ritual purity concerns to sexual acts and religious practices. Biologically evolved emotional reactions against threatening physical substances and situations, selected for their adaptive advantages, feed into culturally constructed conceptions of things not appropriate, and strongly influence moral systems. Fear, originally selected for similar reasons, motivates various avoidance behaviours and protective measures, depending on the social and cultural framework. Empathy, without which a socially complex species like *homo sapiens* would not have survived, not only underlies our capacity to care for offspring and keep together in groups but becomes an important basis for the more inclusive and altruistic expressions of morality that arise in various cultures. I have elsewhere analysed these emotions in more detail and discussed their moral impact in the Pentateuchal legal collections.[22] Although I will focus on empathy and its relationship to prosocial behaviour and altruism in the present article, this does not mean that I consider empathy to be more "moral" than other emotions. However, empathy is good to think with when we try to disentangle – or rather, understand the inevitable blend of – ultimate (biologically evolved) and proximate (culturally constructed) factors in the formation and transformation of moral norms.[23]

Definitions of Altruism

A key issue for this discussion is what we mean by altruism. Does it even exist?[24] Critics of religion in general and concepts of a specific religious morality in parti-

---

[21] The last point was highlighted already by Richard A. Shweder, Manamohan Mahapatra, and Joan G. Miller, "Culture and Moral Development," in *The Emergence of Morality in Young Children* (ed. Jerome Kagan and Sharon Lamb; Chicago, IL: University of Chicago Press, 1987), 1–83.

[22] Kazen, *Emotions.*

[23] Cf. note 9 for literature on ultimate and proximate bases for morality.

[24] For a modern intellectual history of altruism, see Lee Alan Dugatkin, *The Altruism Equation: Seven Scientists Search for the Origins of Goodness* (Princeton, NJ: Princeton University Press, 2006). For a recent defence of altruism, emphasizing action over intention, thoughts, and feelings, see David Sloan Wilson, *Does Altruism Exist? Culture, Genes, and the Welfare of Others* (New Haven, CT: Yale University Press, 2015).

cular tend to say no. As I will argue, this negative reply usually assumes a definition of "genuine" altruism that makes it intrinsically impossible from the start.

Many expressions of prosocial behaviour can be accounted for as kin altruism: We are prepared to forego our own advantages for the sake of individuals genetically related to us. Others qualify as reciprocal altruism, or interaction-based altruism, which expects returns for generous acts, stops if the other defects, and resumes cooperation if the other does reciprocate. Still other expressions may be classified as group altruism or group solidarity, a kind of strategic cooperation, which gives an advantage to all participants. Kin altruism is often dismissed as inauthentic or not "true," but just another sort of selfishness, often with reference to the "selfish gene" concept.[25] But as Martin Zwick and Jeffrey A. Fletcher point out, "[k]inship is the simplest way to get altruism established, not its essence."[26] Reciprocal altruism represents a classic "tit-for-tat" behaviour and is often dismissed as a studied form of selfishness; individuals only engage in generous behaviours as long as they benefit from them. The third type of altruism, sometimes called "mutualism," is often excepted since the cooperation it involves is understood as only strategic and hence not truly self-sacrificing.[27] It is a much discussed question whether such cooperative behaviour can be ultimately explained by selection at the individual level (cooperating individuals outcompeting non-cooperating individuals in the same group), or as the result of group selection (groups with many cooperating

---

[25] This is how Richard Dawkins, *The Selfish Gene* (Oxford: Oxford University Press, 1976), is often read. In the popularized version (and against some of Dawkins' own statements), this is frequently misunderstood to indicate an intrinsic selfishness of human beings. However, the "selfish gene" is just figurative language for the genetic process. It is foul play to require that altruism involve intentionality and disinterested concern, with no benefits to self whatsoever, in order to count as "true" altruism, while using selfishness metaphorically for genetic fitness.

[26] I.e., kinship is an avenue through which human capacity for more extended types of altruism evolved. Martin Zwick and Jeffrey A. Fletcher, "Levels of Altruism," *Biological Theory* 9 (2014): 100–107 (102).

Ironically, the result of this kind of logic is that every attempt to explain altruistic behaviour – whether kin altruism, reciprocal altruism, or mutualism – by natural selection would automatically disprove the existence of that which one tries to explain. This suggests underlying definitions that are untenable. Critics would perhaps object that while behaviour can be seemingly altruistic, underlying motives or ultimate drives are always self-serving. But since every behaviour has evolutionary and biological aspects, this is tantamount to a behaviouristic denial of any human motives or intentions whatsoever, beyond biological instincts and drives. This is a possible stance, but it would make the discussion meaningless.

members have an advantage over groups which had few). The idea of group selection was out of vogue for half a century but is now gaining ground.[28]

If any type of prosocial behaviour which also promotes inclusive fitness[29] is understood more or less as selfishness in disguise, the whole discussion of altruism becomes meaningless; The existence of the object for discussion is made impossible by default.[30] As more than one theorist has pointed out, self or self-interest is the basis for all types of altruism, since it takes a biologically living, feeling, and thinking self in order consciously to do something for others.[31] This requires a sense of belonging, so that the self is by definition somehow involved in the larger group which benefits from the behaviour.

The scope of such a sense of group belonging can be extended almost infinitely, as Frans de Waal has argued, in relation to an experienced sufficiency of resources. But if "true" altruism is defined as acts and attitudes outside and regardless of any such "social" context, it becomes more or less non-human behaviour. There is no point in limiting the concept of altruism to an absolute selflessness, to the point where the self no longer has any needs and no longer is related to any group. Such selves are only fictional creations of Western individualism.

I would thus opt for a broad definition of altruism as prosocial or other-serving attitudes and behaviours that stretch beyond strict limits of self or group identity (kin, tribe, nation, or race), into a wider sense of group belonging. The various ways in which human beings actually acquire such a *widened* sense of belonging is a fascinating topic in itself, for which there is no room here.[32]

The Development of Empathy and Prosocial Behaviour

The most important prerequisite for prosocial behaviour and altruism is the evolution of empathy. Empathy, sympathy, and compassion are often used synonym-

---

[28] For a couple of recent examples, see Samuel Bowles and Herbert Gintis, *A Cooperative Species: Human Reciprocity and Its Evolution* (Princeton, NJ: Princeton University Press, 2011) and Edward O. Wilson, *The Social Conquest of Earth* (New York: Liveright, 2012). Bowles and Gintis use "multi-level selection" interchangeably.

[29] Inclusive fitness, meaning behaviour which promotes one's genetic offspring.

[30] Cf. Robert L. Trivers, "The Evolution of Reciprocal Altruism," *The Quarterly Review of Biology* 46 (1971): 35–57, who plainly (and in my view falsely) states: "Models that attempt to explain altruistic behavior in terms of natural selection are models designed to take the altruism out of altruism" (p. 35).

[31] See for example de Waal, *Good Natured*, 212–214; *Primates and Philosophers*, 161–165; cf. *The Age of Empathy: Nature's Lesson for a Kinder Society* (New York: Broadway Books, 2009).

[32] I am here thinking of the role of awe, meditation, mysticism, and ritual coordination for human cooperation and a widened sense of belonging.

ously in everyday speech. While compassion is usually something one shows in action, and sympathy can be limited to feelings *for* a person, empathy can be used broadly for the emotional response in its various aspects to the plight of others: "an affective response more appropriate to someone else's situation than to one's own."[33]

Empathy has multiple levels. Martin Hoffman discusses five modes of empathic arousal[34] and Stephanie Preston and Frans de Waal provide a slightly different model, again with five categories.[35] In the following I will combine the language of the two schemes (in part) and distinguish between motor mimicry, emotional contagion, emotional matching or direct association, mediated association, and perspective-taking. The first three modes are preverbal, and the empathy aroused is an involuntary affective response. The fourth and fifth modes require a higher cognitive level and depend on the transmission of some information.[36]

This means that, at one end of the scale, empathy is an emotional response which requires little or no reasoning. Says de Waal:

> We're preprogrammed to reach out. Empathy is an automated response over which we have limited control. We can suppress it, mentally block it, or fail to act on it, but except for a tiny percentage of humans – known as psychopaths – no one is emotionally immune to another's situation.[37]

At the other side of the scale, however, human rational capacities facilitate empathic feelings and empathy-induced actions without any close match between the empathizer's and the victim's initial affects.[38] But it is worth noting that the different levels of empathy depend on each other, in a manner for which de Waal uses the image of a Russian doll. Perspective-taking is dependent on acquiring a perspective in the first place, through one's own experiences, through emotional

---

[33] Martin L. Hoffman, "The Contribution of Empathy to Justice and Moral Judgment," in *Empathy and Its Development* (ed. Nancy Eisenberg and Janet Strayer; Cambridge Studies in Social and Emotional Development; Cambridge: Cambridge University Press, 1987), 47–80 (48).

[34] These are: motor mimicry, classic conditioning, direct association based on one's own experience, mediated association based on one's own experience and information from or about the victim, and finally, role- or perspective-taking. Martin L. Hoffman, *Empathy and Moral Development: Implications for Caring and Justice* (Cambridge: Cambridge University Press, 2000), 5.

[35] Preston and de Waal understand empathy within a "Perception-Action Model," which includes a full range of responses, from simple motor mimicry to prosocial behaviour. Their categories are emotional contagion, sympathy, empathy, cognitive empathy, and prosocial behaviours. The last one is focused on action. Preston and de Waal, "Empathy," 2–4, Table 2.

[36] Hoffman, *Empathy*, 5.

[37] De Waal, *Age of Empathy*, 43.

[38] Hoffman, *Empathy*, 5.

development, and through the capacity to mirror others' affects, including reactive crying and motor mimicry. The outer layers thus build upon the inner ones.[39]

In the evolution of *homo sapiens* as a successful social species, two steps have been deemed crucial for the formation of empathy's innermost core: mirror neurons and a theory of mind.

Mirror neurons were first found in experiments on monkeys. They are active in both performing and observing an action. But while they seem to be suited for action imitation, this capacity belongs to a relatively late stage in evolution, which is hardly present in monkeys and only partially in apes.[40] It is likely that mirror neurons did not originally evolve for imitation, but for *understanding* actions performed by others, as well as their emotional states. Studies of humans suggest that mirror mechanisms cause the observer to enact the actions of others inside him/herself and share their emotions, thus transforming what others do and feel into the observer's own experience.[41] It seems that the same neural circuits which are activated by feeling pain are also activated by seeing another person in pain.[42] This would indicate that at the very lowest end of the scale, empathy is based on a sort of analogy to motor mimicry.

The other important step in the formation of empathy is theory of mind, the ability to register or recognize the mental state of others.[43] Humans are not completely unique in being able to recognize what others think and thus represent their

---

[39] De Waal, *Primates and Philosophers*, 37–42 (Figure 4). For another overview of various levels, definitions, and perspectives, see Jean Decety and William Ickes (eds.), *The Social Neuroscience of Empathy* (Cambridge, MA: The MIT Press, 2009).

[40] We are here talking of observing an action and then repeating it afterwards. Monkeys do mirror or reflect simple behaviours, i.e., motor mimicry, as is clear from the research on mirror neurons performed on macaques, which perform imitation of facial imagery.

[41] Laurie Carr *et al.*, "Neural Mechanisms of Empathy in Humans: A Relay from Neural Systems for Imitation to Limbic Areas," *Proceedings of the National Academy of Sciences* 100 (2003): 5497–5502; Marco Iacoboni and Mirella Dapretto, "The Mirror Neuron System and the Consequences of Its Dysfunction," *Nature* 7 (2006): 942–950; Giacomo Rizzolatti and Laila Craighero, "The Mirror-Neuron System," *Annual Review of Neuroscience* 27 (2004): 169–192; idem, "Mirror Neuron: A Neurological Approach to Empathy," in *Neurobiology of Human Values* (ed. Jean-Pierre Changeux *et al.*; Research and Perspectives in Neuroscience; Berlin: Springer, 2005), 107–123.

[42] Giacomo Rizzolatti and Maddalena Fabbri Destro, "Mirror Neurons," *Scholarpedia* 3 (2008): 2055 (http://www.scholarpedia.org/article/Mirror_neurons), with further references to research by T. Singer, M. V. Saarela *et al.*, and V. Gallese *et al.*

[43] De Waal, *Primates and Philosophers*, see especially Appendix B, 69–73; cf. de Waal, *Good Natured*; Peter Gärdenfors, *How Homo Became Sapiens: On the Evolution of Thinking* (Oxford: Oxford University Press, 2003), 83–109.

inner world, but they are far more advanced at this than apes or elephants. Such access to an "*inner* inner world,"[44] from which one can observe one's own inner world and make inferences about others, is necessary for the levels of empathy belonging to the upper end of the scale, mediated association and perspective-taking, for which more advanced cognitive capacities are required.

This multi-layered type of empathy has probably evolved to such an extent in humans because of its adaptive advantage. It contributes greatly to the inclusive fitness of the human species, as it paves the ground generally for prosocial action and particularly for the type of prosocial action that we call altruism. It is functional at all levels: Even a small child reacting to another child at the level of emotional contagion attracts the attention of parents or other adults, and already at the age of two, children begin to distinguish between their own emotions and the emotional state of others and attempt to bring help.[45] Also for reasoning adults, it takes quite some effort to withstand the pull from the lower levels of empathy and overrule them. For doing that it seems that we need other emotions to enter the game.[46]

This means that humanitarian behaviour is based on biological evolution and firmly rooted in the neurobiological constitution of human beings. It is, however, also thoroughly shaped by culture.[47] In fact, even among apes and monkeys, levels of "cultural" shaping of empathic or prosocial behaviour can be observed, for example in rhesus monkeys who learn to practice the peace-making skills of stump-tailed macaques after long periods of interaction and acculturation.[48] With human beings, the particular forms or expressions that the higher and more cognitive levels of empathy take on are context-dependent cultural constructs, which interact with a number of other evolved/cultural emotional concerns, and may restrain even the expressions of more immediate, lower levels of empathy. Prosocial agency and altruism are indeed natural: an evolved, emotionally based capacity in constant negotiation with other such capacities, and always subject to cultural constraints.

---

[44] The expression comes from Gärdenfors, *How Homo Became Sapiens*, 113–114 and elsewhere.

[45] See the examples in Hoffman, *Empathy*, 63–92.

[46] For this, see my discussions in Kazen, *Emotions*.

[47] Cf. Michael Tomasello, *Why We Cooperate?* (Cambridge, MA: Boston Review, 2009).

[48] De Waal, *Good Natured*, 163–208.

Analysis and Application

Examples of In-group Altruism

I will now apply this theoretical discussion in an analysis of biblical texts with pro-social tendencies, seeing whether it can further our understanding of the formation and transformation of moral norms. We will begin with a series of texts displaying altruistic attitudes and behaviours towards an in-group – a kind of kin altruism.

The command to care for immigrants, orphans and widows recurs repeatedly in the legal collections, and first appears in the humanitarian laws in Exod 22:20–26 (ET 21–27). These are part of a larger section of apodictic laws (Exod 22:20 [ET 22:21]–23:19), the second main half of the Covenant Code (Exod 20:22–23:33). Except for the immigrant (v. 20 [21]), which will be addressed in the next section, the categories mentioned are vulnerable in-group members: the orphan and widow (vv. 21–23 [22–24]) we assume, the poor debtor (v. 24 [25]) explicitly so (*et-ʿammî et-heʿānî ʿimmak*), and in the case of taking a cloak in pawn (vv. 25–26 [26–27]), the person is called "neighbour" (*rēaʿ*). Exhortations to practise this kind of in-group altruism are quite common in the ancient world, with similar examples in Hammurabi's law.[49]

What is remarkable in the Covenant Code is the appeal to empathy through a number of rhetorical devices.[50] First (v. 22 [23]), abused widows and orphans are envisaged as crying out to God and God is envisaged as hearing them. God thus responds emotionally to their plight at the lower levels of empathic reaction, which implies that the Israelites addressed by the command ought to do the same. This becomes even more explicit with the debtor (v. 26 [27]), whose cry God will listen to because he is compassionate (*ḥannûn*). Secondly, the text appeals to the higher levels of the recipients' empathic reaction by relying on the cognitive capacity to relate one's own experiences to that of others, or imagine the poor neighbour's feelings based on general knowledge and rational perspective-taking: "it may be your neighbour's only clothing to use as cover; in what else shall that person

---

[49] LH xlvii 59–78; cf. David P. Wright, "The Laws of Hammurabi as a Source for the Covenant Collection (Exodus 20:23–23:19)," *Maarav* 10 (2003): 11–87 (37, 49–50).

[50] Ancient West Asian law collections are often understood as royal *apologiae* and the biblical collections have at times been similarly understood as rhetorical manœuvres serving the interests of the elite by portraying them as benevolent. Cf. Mark Sneed, "Israelite Concern for the Alien, Orphan, and Widow: Altruism or Ideology?" in *Zeitschrift für die alttestamentliche Wissenschaft* III (1999): 498–507. Whether or not such a characterization is accepted, the emotional basis for and impact of these injunctions remain.

sleep?"[51] The bodily experience of freezing is assumed to be universal, so no further explanation of the debtor's situation is needed. Thirdly, in order to reinforce the message, there is a threat, at first explicitly (v. 23 [24]: "I will surely heed their cry; my wrath will burn, and I will kill you with the sword, and your wives shall become widows and your children orphans"),[52] and then implicitly (v. 26 [27]: "I will listen").

The way in which moral norms are here formed by appeals to emotions is conspicuous. Not only is empathy enlisted in its multi-levelled character, but fear is thrown in to strengthen the argument, or rather, the affective force of the imagery. From a rhetorical perspective this is probably strategical in its context since several other emotions would be readily available for countering and negotiating the initial pull of empathic feelings.

For a number of subsequent humanitarian laws in the Covenant Code, an underlying appeal to empathy may be assumed, but it is not explicit on the surface of the text. This is also the case when the Deuteronomic law reuses and further develops the Covenant Code. Neither Deut 10:17–19 nor 24:10–22, which build on the texts from Exodus that were just discussed, retain the same emotional charge. The commands are almost purged from these empathic triggers and turned into drier rules. The exception is Deut 24:15, which reminds recipients that the livelihood of the poor depends on their daily wages, as part of the argument not to withhold them, i.e., without being paid they will have nothing to eat. But the express motivation is that they will cry out to God with the result that their employer will incur guilt (*hāyâ bĕkā ḥēṭ'*).

Although some may find these differences subtle, they may be taken as evidence for different cultural conditions and historical and political contexts. More specifically, the Deuteronomic version of these rules could be understood as part of a process of legal codification and extension of material from the Covenant Code, but with less focus on rhetorical and emotional pragmatics. Although both empathy and fear are enlisted in support of the argument, this is done in a much weaker form compared to the Covenant Code. Hence, in Deuteronomy these humanitarian laws seem to depend more on the recipients' ability for perspective-

---

[51] Biblical texts are generally quoted from the NRSV translation but see note 54.

[52] This is actually a sort of talion (cf. Exod 21:23–24), which in itself depends on a capacity for at least the lower levels of empathic reaction.

taking and less on their gut reactions. Their power is assumed to lie in the divine command.[53]

Reaching Beyond

The texts already discussed also suggest extending prosocial behaviour to another category at the margins, the foreigner. The Covenant Code says: "You shall not wrong or oppress an immigrant (*gēr*), for you were immigrants in the land of Egypt" (Exod 22:20 [ET 22:21]).[54] This command extends prosocial treatment to people beyond the immediate in-group, based on an appeal to the same or similar experience. It is repeated later, with an additional motivation: "you know the heart (*nepeš*) of an immigrant" (23:9), which further underscores the emotional component in such an appeal. The texts speak to the empathy of its recipients in order to include this category with those people who ought to be objects of fair, prosocial, altruistic treatment.

The *gēr* is probably not any foreigner in general, but most likely the resident stranger, the immigrant, neither in-group, nor out-group, but something in between.[55] It has been suggested that here it may apply to the many refugees who needed to be accommodated by the Southern kingdom during and after the Assyrian wars, the fall of Samaria, the siege of Jerusalem, and the conquest of the Shephelah in the late 8th century BCE.[56] This is tied up with the question of what

---

[53] Cf. Carol A. Newsom, "Moral 'Recipes' in Deuteronomy and Ezekiel: Divine Authority and Human Agency," in *Hebrew Bible and Ancient Israel* 6 (2017): 488–509.

[54] The NRSV translates *gēr* with "alien" or "resident alien," since the Hebrew term refers not to foreigners in general, but to an intermediate category. In my discussion, however, I prefer to use "immigrant," which suggests precisely this understanding. I have adapted the NRSV accordingly, here and below.

[55] For discussions of the *gēr* in the different strata of the pentateuchal legal collections, see Jacob Milgrom, *Leviticus 17–22: A New Translation with Introduction and Commentary* (AB 3A; New York: Doubleday, 2000), 1416–1420, 1493–1501; Reinhard Achenbach, "*gēr – nåkhrî – tôshav – zår*: Legal and Sacral Distinctions on Foreigners in the Pentateuch," 29–52; Rainer Albertz, "From Aliens to Proselytes: Non-Priestly and Priestly Legislation Concerning Strangers," 53–69; Christophe Nihan, "Resident Aliens and Natives in the Holiness Legislation," 111–134; all in *The Foreigner and the Law: Perspectives from the Hebrew Bible and the Ancient Near East* (ed. Reinhard Achenbach *et al.*; Wiesbaden: Harrassowitz, 2011). For the *gēr* in Deuteronomy, see also Carly L. Crouch, *The Making of Israel* (SupVT 162; Leiden: Brill, 2014), 216–223.

[56] Archaeological excavations and surveys of the Judean region provide ample evidence for a sudden and extensive expansion of Jerusalem and Judah from the late 8th and through the 7th century BCE; cf. Israel Finkelstein and Neil A. Silberman, *The Bible Unearthed: Archaeology's New Vision of Ancient Israel and the Origin of Its Sacred Texts* (New York: Touchstone, 2002),

the references to Egypt indicate. In the world of the text, they have just left Egypt and are now required to show empathy to other foreigners. Accordingly, these references seemingly appeal to the Israelites' empathy at the level of emotional match or direct association.

But there is an ill fit, because in the Exodus narrative they have been liberated from slavery and extremely harsh treatment. This is the opposite of how they are asked to treat immigrants themselves. The text is, however, composite and the basic material in the Covenant Code is of an earlier date than the Exodus narrative. It is conspicuous that nothing is said in the Covenant Code about the Israelites being *slaves* in Egypt, but rather only being immigrants (*gērîm*).[57] Where Deuteronomy first picks up and rewrites the Covenant Code, the situation is basically the same (10:19), but a reference to the Genesis story (seventy ancestors went down to Egypt) is added, almost as an afterthought (10:22).[58] The *gēr* returns several times in the stereotyped triad of immigrants, orphans and widows.[59] Only in Deut 24:18, 22, do we find references to slavery in the motivation for empathic treatment of immigrants.[60] Such references are probably best seen in light of the long composition history of Deuteronomy and against the background of an evolving Exodus

---

235–246; William M. Schniedewind, "Jerusalem, the Late Judahite Monarchy, and the Composition of the Biblical Texts," in *Jerusalem in Bible and Archaeology: The First Temple Period* (ed. Andrew G. Vaughn and Ann E. Killebrew; Leiden: Brill, 2003), 375–393; Ronny Reich and Eli Shukron, "The Urban Development of Jerusalem in the Late Eighth Century B.C.E.," in *Jerusalem in Bible and Archaeology* (ed. Vaughn and Killebrew), 209–218. Although the term may well refer to displaced Israelites in the Covenant Code, there seems to be a gradual shift of meaning in later strata (through Deuteronomy and the Holiness Code), until the LXX translates the term as proselyte (*prosēlytos*). Cf. Crouch, *The Making of Israel*, 216–223; Milgrom, *Leviticus 17–22*, 1499–1501.

[57] See my discussion in Kazen, *Emotions*, 99–102. The concluding section of (or rather, appendix to) the Covenant Code (Exod 23:20–33), which reflects a conquest narrative and thus relates to the Exodus story, is generally understood as later; for brief references see David P. Wright, *Inventing God's Law: How the Covenant Code of the Bible Used and Revised the Laws of Hammurabi* (Oxford: Oxford University Press, 2009), 499, n. 83. The reference to Egypt in Exod 23:15, with its cross reference to Exod 13:6, can be explained as a later insertion when the Covenant Code was integrated with an Exodus narrative.

[58] See Thomas Römer, *Israels Väter: Untersuchungen zur Väterthematik im Deuteronomium und in der deuteronomistischen Tradition* (OBO 99; Freiburg: Universitätsverlag, 1990), 31–34, with references to a number of scholars (p. 32, nn. 104 and 105), although Römer himself does not find the suggestion of an addition necessary.

[59] E.g., Deut 14:29; 16:11–12, 14; 24:17–22; 26:12–13.

[60] References to slavery in Egypt is also found in Deut 5:15; 15:15; 16:12.

narrative.[61] But initially, in the Covenant Code as well as in the Deuteronomic core, Egypt would not primarily have been a place of slavery but a location where Israelites, according to social memory, would have lived as a non-indigenous population group.[62]

As a result, the appeal to a direct association type of empathy for the immigrant would fit an alternative narrative of Israelite settlement in Egypt – a narrative we no longer have – better than the final form of the narrative, to which these appeals now belong. For the real recipients of these texts, however, we must count on a mediated type of empathy, which relates their social memory to present-day events, and at least in part relies on a capacity for perspective-taking. Here, the hypothesis about an influx of northern refugees, now landless, during the late 8th century BCE, fits well for the Covenant Code. For Deuteronomy we could assume a number of similar contextualizations during its period of formation. Experiences of various types of minority situations, displacements, and losses of land would have been close at hand both during the 7th century BCE and around the exile. Repeated injunctions regarding the immigrant (*gēr*) suggest a movement away from a narrow kin altruism to a more open attitude. To this movement, Deuteronomy adds another emotional component: love. God loves (*'ōhēb*) the immigrant (Deut 10:18). The in-group addressees should do so, too (10:19).

As the post-exilic Holiness Code partly reuses Covenant Code and Deuteronomic material, it also provides instructions about immigrants. Although these are no longer presented in the traditional triad with orphans and widows, they are associated with the poor and are likewise objects of mercy: "You shall not strip your vineyard bare, or gather the fallen grapes of your vineyard; you shall leave them for the poor and the immigrant" (Lev 19:10, NRSV adapted). This is virtually repeated in 23:22. The implication is that these immigrants cannot otherwise provide food for themselves.

---

[61] Today it is quite common to view Deuteronomy's references to Genesis and the patriarchal stories as secondary, understanding Deuteronomy to take the exodus as its point of departure; cf. Römer, *Väter;* and Konrad Schmid, *Genesis and the Moses Story: Israel's Dual Origins in the Hebrew Bible* (Siphrut: Literature and Theology of the Hebrew Scriptures 3; Winona Lake: Eisenbrauns, 2010), 67–69. What I suggest here, however, is that early references to being immigrants in Egypt did not assume slavery, and hence these references do not reflect a developed form of the exodus tradition.

[62] This is also more in accord with historically plausible scenarios of cyclic migration of Asiatics into the Egyptian delta area. See for example Finkelstein and Silberman, *Bible Unearthed*, 48–71.

The Holiness Code seemingly builds further on Deuteronomy's injunction (10:18–19) to love the immigrant. A central passage (Lev 19:33–34) reads:

> When an immigrant (*gēr*) resides with you in your land, you shall not oppress the immigrant. The immigrant who resides with you shall be to you as the citizen (*'ezrāḥ*) among you; you shall love (*'āhabtā*) the immigrant as yourself, for you were immigrants in the land of Egypt: I am the LORD your God. (NRSV adapted)

The command to love immigrants is again motivated by a similar experience ("you were immigrants in the land of Egypt"), but sharpened by the addition "as yourself," which underscores an emotional and associative type of empathy, beyond mere perspective-taking. In addition, the Israelites are explicitly told to regard the immigrant just like one of them, like a citizen (Lev 19:34). This explains why the injunction to love the immigrant is parallel to the previous command about the neighbour: "love your neighbour (*rēʿākā*) as yourself" (Lev 19:18). It represents a further extension of kin altruism, by integrating outsiders and making them part of the in-group, and it is particular to the Holiness Code.[63]

This section of the Holiness Code incidentally came to play an important role in the formation of early Jewish moral norms, and through its reception and refraction in the Jesus tradition (Sermon on the Mount) also in early Christian transferral and transformation of these norms within a Greco-Roman setting. It promotes a relatively inclusive type of altruism, by construing an "extended family," a sense of kin which goes beyond traditional limits. The emotional appeal rests on the sense of close relationships. Most of the prosocial commandments refer to the "neighbour" (Lev 19:13, 15, 16, 17, 18), thereby creating or reinforcing a sense of family. The immigrant is then brought into this community.[64] This section also suggests love of adversaries:

> You shall not hate in your heart anyone of your kin (*'āḥtkā*); you shall reprove your neighbour (*'āmttekā*), or you will incur guilt yourself. You shall not take vengeance or

---

[63] The emphasis on equal treatment is particular to the Holiness Code and goes together with a repeated claim that various holiness laws are valid for immigrants and supposed to be followed by them to the same extent as by native Israelites. See Lev 17:8, 10, 12, 13, 15; 18:26; 20:2; 22:18; 24:16, 22, and further in Num 9:14; 15:14–16, 26, 29–30; 19:10; 35:15. Cf. the Passover narrative in Exod 12:19, 48–49. For a discussion of how these rules relate to the social and political circumstances surrounding the Holiness Code, as well as possible identities of the *gērîm*, see articles in *The Foreigner and the Law* (ed. Achenbach), and comments in Milgrom, *Leviticus 17–22* (cf. n. 55, above).

[64] There is one conspicuous difference: foreigners and immigrants may become eternal slaves of Israelites, without the year of release applying, while Israelite slaves of resident immigrants must be freed (Lev 25:35–55). Cf. Nihan, "Resident Aliens," 123–124.

bear a grudge against any of your people (*běnê ʿammekā*), but you shall love your neigh-bour (*rēʿākā*) as yourself: I am the LORD. (NRSV adapted)

Again, kin relationship at family, class/clan, and tribal levels (*ʾāḥîkā*, literally "your brother"; *ʿămîtekā*, literally "your associate / relation"; *běnê ʿammekā*, literally "the sons of your people") is invoked rhetorically to motivate and emotionally trig-ger an altruistic attitude and increased prosocial behaviour beyond what could otherwise be expected, based on customary law and talion. The familial language invites multileveled empathic feelings, drawing on experiences of personal rela-tionships.

This is certainly not an example of unlimited altruism, not even of "enemy love" proper, and within the broader context of the Holiness Code it is restricted by requirements of conformity, as will be discussed below. This is nevertheless how altruism expands: by including those who were previously regarded as out-group within the limits of the in-group, sharing resources and helping behaviours within a widening circle.[65] The ways in, and the extent to which, such expansion is deemed reasonable depends on context and is a matter of cultural construction, but the biological basis for this to take place is provided by evolution, through processes of adaptation, which are geared towards inclusive fitness.[66]

Extended Kinship and Non-revenge

The injunction in the Holiness Code to love immigrants *as oneself* and *forego re-venge* may seem to go against human natural propensities. The urges to favour or prioritize one's own kin, as well as to retaliate, are certainly innate survival strate-gies, without which the human species would have become extinct. Kin altruism, however, does not strictly require a genetic relationship, as researchers have repeat-edly pointed out. Although kin selection lies at the roots of the evolution of altru-ism, kin recognition is quite unstable in nature and, in actual practice, kin altruism often works no more precisely than by the recognition of group belonging (nur-ture kinship). This is why the extension of altruism by "fictive kin" is efficient.[67]

---

[65] On this, see Preston and de Waal, 212–214; de Waal, *Primates and Philosophers*, 161–165.

[66] See note 29.

[67] Maximilian P. Holland, "Social Bonding and Nurture Kinship: Compatibility Between Cultural and Biological Approaches" (PhD diss., University of London: London School of Eco-nomic and Political Science, Department of Sociology, 2004). Cf. David M. Schneider, *A Cri-tique of the Study of Kinship* (Ann Arbor, MI: The University of Michigan Press, 1984); Wilson, *Social Conquest*, 49–56.

Moreover, the tendency to forego revenge, which some call the "forgiveness instinct,"[68] is a function of kin altruism as it expands into group altruism. The valuable relationships hypothesis claims, based on experiments with primates, that quick reconciliation between individuals has evolved among social species to preserve relationships of crucial importance. Group-living organisms that were willing to forgive group members simply had better chances to survive than those who did not, since they were more successful at cooperation.[69] Also, forgiveness in close relationships lowers levels of anxious tension. This means that forgiveness, like revenge, is context-sensitive and depends on how we experience our relationship with the perpetrator. Forgiveness, just like revenge, can give emotional satisfaction. When empathy enters the game, it plays on the side of forgiveness, and may seriously disturb and outbid the satisfaction gained from revenge.[70]

The Holiness Code's strategy of expanding fictive kinship would have effectively transformed moral norms by appealing to empathy and thus extending the scope of a biologically based altruism with the help of cultural modifiers. The historical context of a small emerging temple state, trying to rebuild national identity by emphasizing unity and cohesion, and using familial language, seems like a good fit for this text. It is reasonable to assume a society that was basically kin- or clan-based, but at the same time diverse, including residents and immigrants of various origins, some of whom were non-Israelites. The Holiness Code injunctions reflect a strategy for holding them together in peaceful cooperation.[71]

The expansion of empathy to the effect that adversaries or foreigners may be included, and revenge overridden, is not an overly common motif in the Hebrew

---

[68] From the subtitle of Michael McCullough, *Beyond Revenge: The Evolution of the Forgiveness Instinct* (San Francisco, CA: Jossey-Bass, 2008).

[69] Frans de Waal and Angeline van Roosmalen, "Reconciliation and Consolation Among Chimpanzees," *Behavioral Ecology and Sociobiology* 5 (1979): 55–66; Filippo Aureli and Colleen Schaffner, "Causes, Consequences and Mechanisms of Reconciliation: The Role of Cooperation," in *Cooperation in Primates and Humans: Mechanisms and Evolution* (ed. Peter M. Kappeler and Carel P. van Schaik; Berlin: Springer, 2006) 121–135; McCullough, *Beyond Revenge*, 124–127. One of the most conspicuous experiments shows how long-tailed macaques that were taught to cooperate in order to obtain food experienced a doubling of post-conflict reconciliations. Marina Cords and Sylvie Thurnheer, "Reconciling with Valuable Partners by Long-tailed Macaques," *Ethology* 93 (1993): 315–325; McCullough, *Beyond Revenge*, 126.

[70] McCullough, *Beyond Revenge*, 147–154.

[71] Nihan identifies the *gērîm* as people who do not own land, and suggests they included not only migrant workers, but also "wealthy merchant families, foreign soldiers, members of the Achaemenid administration, and so on" (Nihan, "Resident Aliens," 132). He discusses their legal as well as their sacral status.

Bible. In addition to the Holiness Code, a couple of interesting examples with references to kinship are found in narrative texts from (or compiled during) the Persian and Hellenistic periods. In Genesis 32–33, Esau foregoes his expected revenge on Jacob.[72] Jacob interprets the approaching army of four hundred as signalling Esau's intended retaliation and responds (32:21 [ET 32:20]) by sending gifts in order to "effect removal before him" or simply, "appease his anger" (*'ăkappĕrāh pānâw*).[73] Esau, however, foregoes all revenge regardless of any gifts (33:9). The narrative's reconciliation between two brothers typically illustrates the valuable relationships hypothesis. In the chronicler's narrative (2 Chr 28:5–15),[74] the prophet Oded convinces the Israelites in Samaria to return Judean war prisoners with clothes, shoes, and food, after they had been captured in war. The argument is expressed with filial language ("your brothers"; *'ăḥêkem*). Empathy and non-revenge behaviours towards enemies are realized as an extension of kin altruism.

While revenge is a common topic in prophetic literature, the foregoing of revenge is uncommon. God is an avenger, although not always punishing the people to the full extent that they deserve. The late book of Jonah is somewhat of an anomaly, as it tweaks the prophetic genre into a novella, which problematizes the

---

[72] Dating the details of the Jacob cycle today is tricky. The material is probably non-P. See Albert de Pury, "The Jacob Story and the Beginning of the Formation of the Pentateuch," in *Farewell to the Yahwist? The Composition of the Pentateuch in Recent European Interpretation* (ed. Thomas B. Dozeman and Konrad Schmid; Symposium Series 34; Atlanta: Society of Biblical Literature, 2006), 51–72. Pre-exilic origins are reasonable, but for much of the Jacob-Esau narrative the 6th century BCE conflicts between Judah and Edom seem a plausible background, and an exilic or early Persian period setting for the shaping of this section is possible. Cf. discussions in Thomas Römer, "B. Der Pentateuch," in *Die Entstehung des Alten Testaments* (ed. Walter Dietrich et al.; Theologische Wissenschaft: Sammelwerk für Studium und Beruf 1; new ed.; Stuttgart: Kohlhammer, 2014), 53–166 (108–110); and Diana Edelman, "Genesis: A Composition for Construing a Homeland of the Imagination for Elite Scribal Circles or for Educating the Illiterate?" in *Writing the Bible: Scribes, Scribalism and Script* (ed. Thomas Römer and Philip R. Davies; London: Routledge, 2014), 46–66.

[73] Cf. Yitzhaq Feder, *Blood Expiation in Hittite and Biblical Ritual: Origins, Context, and Meaning* (Writings from the Ancient World Supplement Series 2; Atlanta, GA: Society of Biblical Literature, 2011), 171–173.

[74] A conventional date for Chronicles is around 400 BCE, but many scholars prefer a later date in the late 4th or early 3rd century. See Gary N. Knoppers, *I Chronicles 1–9: A New Translation with Introduction and Commentary* (Anchor Bible: New York: Doubleday, 2004), 101–117. For a more conservative date, see Ralph W. Klein, *1 Chronicles: A Commentary* (Hermeneia; Minneapolis, MN: Fortress, 2006), 13–16.

conventional prophetic oracle of doom.[75] In the end, God proves himself to be more compassionate and forgiving than his own prophets. Although the Ninevites are not portrayed as enemies, the assumption of the text's recipients would have been that they were neither compatriots nor friends.[76] The motivation for God's leniency is implicitly empathic, but in laconic disguise: "Should I not feel pity (*ḥûs*) for Nineveh, the big city, where over one hundred and twenty thousand people live who do not know the difference between right and left – and many animals?" (Jonah 4:11). The statement is a reproof not only of the narrative's prophet, but also of conceptions of God as overly revengeful, as well as of human ideals of revenge.

The extension of empathy and altruism beyond factual or fictive family, occasionally surfaces in poetic literature. Proverbs 20:22 suggests that human beings should forego revenge and trust God who will save (*yoša' lāk*). However, the implication may be that God will take revenge on one's behalf.[77] Proverbs 24:17–18 warns people not to rejoice over an enemy who falls or stumbles, because God might not like *Schadenfreude*, and may turn his wrath away from the enemy. To desire revenge seems to be legitimate, but one should be modest about it.[78] Proverbs 25:21–22 contains an invitation to give bread and water to an enemy, but the cryptic firecoals upon the enemy's head, which such action effects, may again suggest that Proverbs does not attest to an expansion of empathy or altruism. Rather, it points only to a certain understanding of what is appropriate for human beings to effect on their own and what should be left to God.[79] Proverbs hardly takes the

---

[75] See the introductory discussion in Uriel Simon, *Jonah* (The JPS Bible Commentary; Philadelphia, PA: The Jewish Publication Society, 1999), vii–xliii, which places Jonah safely in the Second Temple period, as well as the arguments of André Lacocque and Pierre-Emmanuel Lacocque, *Le complexe de Jonas* (Paris: CERF, 1989), 51–52, for a date after Haggai, Zechariah, and Chronicles, based on the "decentralized universalism" of the book.

[76] Cf. the very different attitude found in the introduction to the book of Nahum.

[77] Michael V. Fox, *Proverbs 10–31: A New Translation with Introduction and Commentary* (AYB 18B; New Haven, CT & London: Yale University Press, 2009), 673–674. Cf. also Prov 24:28–29.

[78] Or, perhaps, the abstention from *Schadenfreude* is the best way to maximize divine revenge; cf. Fox, *Proverbs 10–31*, 750–751.

[79] For a comprehensive account of the history of translation and interpretation of this passage, see Stanislav Segert, "Live Coals Heaped on the Head," in *Love and Death in the Ancient Near East: Essays in Honor of Marvin H. Pope* (ed. John H. Marks and Robert M. Good; Guilford, CT: Four Quarters Publishing Company, 1987), 159–164. For a discussion of forgiveness and revenge in Proverbs, see Gordon M. Zerbe, *Non-Retaliation in Early Jewish and New Testament Texts: Ethical Themes in Social Contexts* (JSPSup 13; Sheffield: Sheffield Academic Press,

extension of kin altruism and the foregoing of revenge any further, when compared to legal and narrative texts.

From Hebrew to Greek

Israel's increasing interaction with the surrounding world, and with Hellenism in particular, provides a context in which ideas of an extended altruism and the foregoing of revenge take somewhat new directions. One partial explanation for this development is the translation of Hebrew scriptures into Greek and the emergence of new Jewish Greek scriptures. The transition from Hebrew to Greek goes together with a shift in the understanding of empathy, as well as a shift in the way God was conceptualized.[80]

Several scholars have argued that the Israelite understanding of being compassionate (*raḥûm*, *ḥannûn*) in general, and of divine benevolence (*ḥesed*) in particular, underwent a development during the Second Temple period. Greek terms, like *oiktirmos*, and especially the frequently employed *eleos*, were associated with inner emotions to a larger extent than their Hebrew counterparts, which carried notions of attitude and action. The divine favour (*ḥesed*) towards God's own covenant people was increasingly understood in terms of pity.[81]

At the same time, Hellenistic notions of transcendence and universalism blended with emerging Israelite monotheism. Greek gods were rarely compassionate, and an evolving Hellenistic concept of divine transcendence gave little room for gods moved by passions.[82] The Israelite God, in contrast, seems to undergo a development, in which covenant-based loyalty and benevolence, understood as both active and affective compassion, were combined with an extension in the scope of divine concern. One could plausibly interpret this process as an expansion of divine empathy towards a broader altruism, based on a widened sense of kin, as one God is becoming the father of all humanity. An emotionally laden compassion thus established itself as constitutive of the divine nature, and human beings were

---

1993), 35–39. Zerbe suggests a difference in attitude towards enemies (as in the texts discussed above) and towards friends and neighbours (i.e., kin, as in Prov 10:12; 12:16; 17:9; and 19:11).

[80] David Konstan, *Pity Transformed* (London: Duckworth, 2001); Françoise Mirguet, *An Early History of Compassion: Emotion and Imagination in Hellenistic Judaism* (Cambridge: Cambridge University Press, 2017).

[81] Jan Joosten, "חסד 'bienveillance' et ἔλεος 'pitié': Réflexions sur une equivalence lexicale dans la Septante," in *"Car c'est l'amour qui me plait, non le sacrifice...": Recherche sur Osée 6:6 et son interpretation juive et chrétienne* (ed. Eberhard Bons; SupJSJ 88; Leiden: Brill, 2004), 25–42; Mirguet, *Compassion*, 64–108.

[82] Konstan, *Pity*, 105–124.

expected to emulate this attitude, truly in line with Israelite holiness theology, at least ideally.

This is the context reflected in Yeshua ben Sira, where we find theological conclusions and motivations for an extended altruism and the foregoing of revenge.[83] The following texts are not extant in the Hebrew *Vorlage*, but only in the Greek text.

> Like a drop of water from the sea and a grain of sand, so are a few years among the days of eternity. That is why the Lord is patient with them and pours out his mercy (*eleos*) upon them. He sees and recognizes that their end is miserable; therefore he grants them forgiveness (*exilasmon*) all the more. The compassion (*eleos*) of human beings is for their neighbours (*ton plēsion autou*), but the compassion (*eleos*) of the Lord is for every living thing (*epi pasan sarka*). He rebukes and trains and teaches them, and turns them back, as a shepherd his flock.[84]

> The vengeful (*ho ekdikōn*) will face the Lord's vengeance (*ekdikēsin*), for he keeps a strict account of their sins. Forgive your neighbour the wrong he has done (*aphes adikēma tōi plēsion sou*), and then your sins will be pardoned when you pray. Does anyone harbour anger against another, and expect healing from the Lord? If one has no mercy (*eleos*) toward another like himself (*ep' anthrōpon homoion autōi*), can he then seek pardon for his own sins?[85]

For ben Sira, the vulnerability (short life, miserable death) of human beings induces empathy or mercy (*eleos*) in God, of a kind that is both emotional and universal, since it is directed towards every living thing (*epi pasan sarka*). This point contrasts human mercy, which is directed only towards one's neighbour (*ton plēsion autou*).[86] For this reason, God grants forgiveness (*exilasmon*). Perhaps we could say that the limitations of human kin or group altruism are understood to correspond to the very limitations that surround human life on the whole, while an empathic concern for all creation is envisaged as a divine capacity.

At the same time, ben Sira expects human behaviour to accommodate to God's. Divine revenge (*ekdikēsis*) figures here too, but as a response to vengeful humans. Forgiving the wrongdoings (*adikēma*) of one's neighbour (*plēsion*) is seen

---

[83] The Hebrew version is usually dated to around 180 BCE, and the Greek translation some decades later.

[84] Sirach 18:10–13, NRSV.

[85] Sirach 28:1–4, NRSV.

[86] Cf. Aristotle (*Rhet.* 2.8), who reserves human *eleos* for the *homoioi* (those who are similar, peers, kin), although he makes an exception for close family, since he thinks we then react as if we were in danger ourselves, rather than with pity. See Konstan, *Pity*, 111–112. For ben Sira, too, similarity (*anthrōpon homoion autōi*), and hence mercy, primarily seem to refer to the neighbour (*plēsion*), but a wider application is possible.

as a prerequisite for obtaining divine forgiveness. Human and divine mercy (*eleos*) are like corresponding vessels.

Although ben Sira does not explicitly demand more from human beings than an empathic behaviour towards the "neighbour," the divine example and the characterization of the object of mercy as "a human being like you" (*anthrōpon homoion autōi*), could be taken to constitute a challenge to extend altruism beyond the borders of kin, clan, and group. There is an implication of *imitatio Dei* here, which harks back to the pre-exilic Covenant Code, which first challenges human empathy by referring to divine feelings. The decisive point, then, is how God is envisaged, and to what extent divine empathy and altruism reach beyond the bounds of the in-group in the author's imagination. Altruism, based as it is on biologically evolved empathy, ultimately turns out to be a potentially unrestricted capacity of the divine mind, as it is envisaged by a Hellenistic period Jewish author, in a context and at a time when the Israelite God goes more universal than ever before. Human beings are challenged but are not expected to be able to follow all the way.

Limitations and Possibilities of Emotional Ethics

How far human beings can follow the divine example depends, of course, on the intricate interplay between ultimate, evolutionary conditions and cultural, contextual construals. Emotions of various kinds are crucial all along this process. A number of empathy-blocking strategies can be observed, in which other emotions are enlisted to negotiate, contradict, and counteract altruistic attitudes and prosocial behaviours that would otherwise have been an option.

In spite of the concern for immigrants, at least of a particular kind, Deuteronomy displays an unrelenting attitude to Ammonites and Moabites (Deut 23:4–7 [ET 3–6]). They may never become part of the people, even after ten generations. This is motivated by their hostile behaviour towards the Israelites in the desert. Because of this, Israelites are forbidden to ever seek their peace and prosperity. Genesis adds an emotional component to reinforce the Israelites' disassociation from these ethnic groups: They stem from the incestuous union between Lot and his daughters (Gen 19:30–38). Disgust and resentment together would perhaps prevent empathy from taking over. For Egyptians and Edomites, however, other rules apply (Deut 23:8–9 [7–8]). They must not be abhorred (*lo'-tĕta'ēb*), implying that disgust would otherwise have been the appropriate feeling, as for the previously mentioned ethnic groups, and their third generation offspring can be integrated. The motivation for the Edomite is filial: He is your brother (*'āḥîkā*). For Egyptians, it is the shared experience of being a foreigner.

These groups probably represent live concerns at the time of the composition or compilation of the text. It is different with the list of six foreign nations to be exterminated: the Amorites, Hittites, Perizzites, Canaanites, Hivites, and Jebusites of the Covenant Code (Exod 23:23–33),[87] a list complemented by a seventh, the Girgashites, in Deuteronomy (7:1–5; cf. 20:10–18). Fear and disgust are explicitly enlisted as empathy-blockers. Although none of these groups were live threats when these texts were shaped, and few were even in existence,[88] the stereotyped list with its harsh and hateful instructions for genocide would have exerted a continued influence towards ethnocentrism and xenophobia.[89]

The attitude of the Holiness Code may at first sight look much more integrating. While this is to some extent true, immigrants, as a partially integrated outgroup, are expected to follow Israelite laws in most regards. There is a sharp contrast to the real outgroup, however: Those who do not follow the holiness laws are cut out,[90] whether natives or immigrants,[91] just like former inhabitants were expelled for their false practices.[92]

And as a counterweight to the tendencies we have noted towards more extended forms of altruism in texts from the Persian and Hellenistic periods, the narrowing attitudes found in the Ezra–Nehemiah corpus can be invoked (Ezra 9–10). Here the various lists of foreign nations from the just-mentioned legal collections are meshed (Ezra 9:1), serving as motivation for Ezra to repudiate and revoke all marriages between Judaean returnees and any people of uncertain descent. The "holy seed" (9:2) has been intermingled or sullied (*hit'ārbû*) by the impurity of the people of the land (*běniddat 'ammê hā'ărāṣôt*), who by their abominations (*bětô'ăbōtêhem*) have made it an impure land (*'ereṣ niddâ*) (9:11; cf. v. 14).

---

[87] This section is probably a late addition to the Covenant Code. See note 57 above.

[88] Billie Jean Collins, "The Bible, The Hittites, and the Construction of the 'Other'," in *Tabularia Hethaeorum: Hethitologische Beiträge Silvin Košak zum 65. Geburtstag* (ed. Detlev Groddek and Marina Zorman; Wiesbaden: Harrassowitz, 2007), 153–161. Cf. J. van Seters, "The Term 'Amorite' and 'Hittite' in the Old Testament," *Vetus Testamentum* 22 (1972): 64–81.

[89] Cf. John J. Collins, "The Zeal of Phinehas: The Bible and the Legitimation of Violence," *Journal of Biblical Literature* 122 (2003): 3–21.

[90] I.e., they are subject to the *karet* penalty. For a discussion of various interpretations of the *karet*, see Yitzhaq Feder, "Purity and Sancta Desecration in Ritual Law: A Durkheimian Perspective," in *The Oxford Handbook of Biblical Law* (ed. Pamela Barmash; Oxford: Oxford University Press, 2019), 101–117.

[91] Lev 17:10; 18:29; 20:2; 24:16; cf. Num 15:30.

[92] Lev 20:22–24.

Deep disgust is enlisted and serves as an empathy-blocking strategy *par excellence*. The texts exemplify that not only empathy and altruism, but all other emotions and action tendencies based on innate dispositions, are shaped and gain their momentum and specific implementation against the background of particular historical and social contexts.[93]

It is precisely this combination of, and interaction between, biology and culture, which also makes further development in altruistic directions possible, as contexts and conditions change. The tendencies we have seen in ben Sira find their continuation in other Jewish Greek texts, such as the *Letter of Aristeas, Joseph and Aseneth*,[94] and in Jewish-Christian texts, such as the *Testaments of the Twelve Patriarchs* (especially *T. Zeb.*), with their many injunctions to non-revenge and forgiveness,[95] and the similarly basically Jewish sayings source (Q) behind the Gospels of Matthew and Luke, which provided the gist of the prosocial and altruistic instructions in the Sermon on the Mount.[96] This part of the story, however, falls outside of the scope of the present study.

Conclusion

I have argued that morality is a developing cultural construct, dependent on innate capacities, which have evolved because they gave the human species adaptive advantages during the course of evolution. Among these capacities, we find a number

---

[93] On this point, cf. the absolutely contradictory viewpoints regarding cultic participation and sacrifice by foreigners in Ezek 44:6–9 (no foreigners in the sanctuary) and Isa 56:1–8 (sacrifices of covenant-keeping foreigners accepted). For a discussion, see Achenbach, *"gēr,"* 38–40; cf. Volker Haarmann, "'Their Burnt Offerings and their Sacrifices Will Be Accepted on my Altar' (Isa 56:7): Gentile Yhwh-Worshipers and their Participation in the Cult of Israel," in *The Foreigner and the Law* (ed. Achenbach), 157–171.

[94] See Zerbe, *Non-Retaliation*, 49–105.

[95] See Zerbe, *Non-Retaliation*, 136–160, 176–210; Mirguet, *Compassion*, 49–57. The hope of reconstructing a Jewish *Grundschrift* behind the present Christian form of the *Testaments* is entertained by few scholars today. However, the type of paraenesis displayed is just as Jewish as it is "Christian." For a research summary, see Robert A. Kugler, *The Testaments of the Twelve Patriarchs* (Guides to Apocrypha and Pseudepigrapha; Sheffield: Sheffield Academic Press, 2001), 11–40.

[96] The (hypothetical) sayings source (Q) behind the *logia* common to Matthew and Luke is disputed but accepted by a majority of scholars as the simplest solution for explaining some obvious literary dependencies. The early Jesus-followers who produced this collection would by all means have been part of an inner-Jewish movement. For an introduction to Q, see John S. Kloppenborg, *The Earliest Gospel: An Introduction to the Original Stories and Sayings of Jesus* (Louisville, KY: WJK Press, 2008).

of emotions, which provide some of the underpinnings for morality. Moral norms are formed and transformed through interaction between these evolved, biologically based reactions and cultural, contextually dependent patterns.

In this article I have focused on empathy, with its potential for an expanding altruism, but without claiming it to be the only important emotion for the development of human morality and moral norms. We have seen that expressions of empathy in the Hebrew Bible to a high degree depend on an innate capacity for empathic emotions, which can be triggered and invoked at multiple levels, from mimicry and emotional contagion to various types of association and perspective-taking. Contextual factors are crucial for deciding at which level(s) empathy is triggered.

We have also found that, in most of the texts where empathy is expressed and altruistic tendencies are displayed, this results in a type of in-group altruism, whether narrowly focused on kin or more broadly on a larger group. However, it seems that kin altruism is just the springboard for a natural expansion of empathy's sphere and the scope of altruistic attitudes and behaviours. Altruism can be expanded to reach beyond previous borders by extending the sense of relatedness. Kin language can be used rhetorically to influence people to embrace a wider group of people in their community. Even obvious out-groups may at times be incorporated in this way and counted among the in-group.

In real life there are limits. These, however, are also emotionally based and culturally situated. The limiting texts discussed above, with their empathy-blocking strategies, do not necessarily suggest that altruism is a utopian idea. They can rather be read as evidence of the crucial role played by people's appraisal of a given context. The measures deemed necessary for the welfare of kin or of the group depend on individual appraisals of the situation, including a variety of emotional responses.

As we have pointed out, not only empathy, but also several other emotions may be seen as linked to welfare, and thus as important for the formation and transformation of moral norms. The limiting effect of emotions like disgust and fear can in a given context turn out to be protective or counterproductive, contributing to or counteracting the welfare of the larger group. The expanding role of altruism in the formation and transformation of moral norms, attitudes, and behaviour, as reflected in the biblical texts, is intimately tied up with emotionally-laden appraisals of the situation, and the biblical authors, like their addressees, differ in their judgments. Their biological conditions and innate emotional capacities are the same. But their cultural contexts and formative environments differ. Which way these authors choose to go depends ultimately on how they process their experiences of themselves and of others, how they envisage an overarching or universal perspective, and how they relate these to each other. Altruism, then, remains a divine potential which human beings can tap into. This is close to where biology gets us, too.

Acknowledgement: The research for this article was partly funded by the Swedish Research Council, grant nr. 2016-02319.

Viewing Oneself through Others' Eyes

Shame between Biology and Culture in Biblical Texts

> A further problem presented by the affections of soul is this: are they all affections of the complex of body and soul, or is there any one among them peculiar to the soul by itself? To determine this is indispensable but difficult. If we consider the majority of them, there seems to be no case in which the soul can act or be acted upon without involving the body; e.g. anger, courage, appetite, and sensation generally. Thinking seems the most probable exception; but if this too proves to be a form of imagination or to be impossible without imagination, it too requires a body as a condition of its existence. If there is any way of acting or being acted upon proper to soul, soul will be capable of separate existence; if there is none, its separate existence is impossible. ... It therefore seems that all the affections of soul involve a body-passion, gentleness, fear, pity, courage, joy, loving, and hating; in all these there is a concurrent affection of the body. (Aristotle, *On the Soul* 403a)[1]

> Let shame (αἰσχύνη) then be defined as a kind of pain or uneasiness in respect of misdeeds, past, present, or future, which seem to tend to bring dishonor; and shamelessness (ἀναισχυντία) as contempt and indifference in regard to these same things. If this definition of shame (αἰσχύνη) is correct, it follows that we are ashamed (αἰσχύνεσθαι) of all such misdeeds as seem to be disgraceful (αἰσχρά), either for ourselves or for those whom we care for. (Aristotle, *Rhetorics* 1383b)[2]

There is little consensus on what emotions really are. Are they feelings, motivations, or evaluations? Not only do evolutionary biologists, neuroscientists, psychologists, and philosophers differ in perspective, but they also disagree within their own guilds, at times vehemently. As Andrea Scarantino points out, in *The Handbook of Emotions*, "we are apparently not much closer to reaching consensus

---

[1] Translation from John Alexander Smith, *The Works of Aristotle: De Anima* (Oxford: Clarendon, 1931).

[2] Translation from John Henry Freese, *Aristotle: The "Art" of Rhetoric* (London: William Heinemann, 1926).

on what emotions are than we were in Ancient Greece."[3] Nevertheless, Scarantino lists fifteen characteristics that are acknowledged by most emotion theorists. The list will not be rehearsed here, except for the third and the fourth point: there are evolutionary explanations for at least some emotions, or their components and emotions are generally affected by sociocultural factors.[4]

This may seem commonplace enough, but for those of us who study emotional expressions in ancient cultures through ancient texts, a keen awareness of the interaction between biological underpinnings and cultural constructions is crucial to avoid at least the worst forms of anachronisms and generalisations.

In this article I will focus on the emotion of shame in the Bible, but I will largely leave the traditional discussion of a Mediterranean honour-shame culture aside. Instead, I will discuss expressions of shame in biblical texts, and I will relate my observations to the biological, evolutionary, and social functions of shame as an embodied emotion and to the ways in which emotional shame is culturally shaped, interpreted, and exploited. As will become clear, our concept of shame only partly overlaps with ancient constructs and terminologies, such as Hebrew בּוֹשׁ, בּוּשָׁה, or בֹּשֶׁת, together with word stems like חפר, כלם, and חרף, with which בּוֹשׁ is often juxtaposed and paralleled, and Greek αἰδώς or αἰσχύνη together with their corresponding verbs and compounds. This fact requires attention and careful analysis, something that has been amply demonstrated by scholars like Douglas Cairns, David Konstan, and Yael Avrahami, to name a few, similarly to what for example David Konstan, Jan Joosten, and Françoise Mirguet have done with regard to pity.[5]

---

[3] Andrea Scarantino, "The Philosophy of Emotions and Its Impact on Affective Science," in *Handbook of Emotions*, 4th ed. (ed. Lisa Feldman Barrett, Michael Lewis, and Jeanette Haviland-Jones; New York: Guilford, 2016), 3–48 (37).

[4] Scarantino, *"Philosophy,"* 37.

[5] Douglas L. Cairns, AIDŌS: *The Psychology and Ethics of Honour and Shame in Ancient Greek Literature* (Oxford: Clarendon, 1993); idem, "Honour and Shame: Modern Controversies and Ancient Values," *Critical Quarterly* 53 (2011): 23–41; David Konstan, *Pity Transformed* (London: Duckworth, 2001); idem, *The Emotions of the Ancient Greeks: Studies in Aristotle and Classical Literature* (Toronto: University of Toronto Press, 2006); Yael Avrahami, "בושׁ in the Psalms—Shame or Disappointment?" *Journal for the Study of the Old Testament* 34 (2010): 295–313; Jan Joosten, "חסד 'bienveillance' et ἔλεος 'pitié': Réflexions sur une equivalence lexicale dans la Septante," in *"Car c'est l'amour qui me plait, non le sacrifice …": Recherche sur Osée 6:6 et son interpretation juive et chrétienne* (ed. E. Bons; SupJSJ 88; Leiden: Brill, 2004), 25–42; Françoise Mirguet, *An Early History of Compassion: Emotion and Imagination in Hellenistic Judaism* (Cambridge: Cambridge University Press, 2017).

Aware of this, I will outline a variety of emotional patterns and relate them to the biological and psychological emotion complex of which shame is part, the shame family of emotions. I will pay special attention to ways in which shame is part of a social web of relationships, in particular to patterns of dominance and subordination. I will try to be aware of aspects of mutualism and hierarchy, power, and deference. The first step, however, is to look at the development of shame as one of a cluster of self-conscious emotions.

The Development of Shame

The field of human emotions is sometimes divided into three types. Other-condemning emotions include contempt, anger, and disgust, and guard the moral order. Other-praising emotions include awe, elevation, and gratitude, and respond to good deeds. Self-conscious emotions include shame, embarrassment, guilt, and pride, and constrain individual behaviour in a social context.[6]

Another way for theorists is to distinguish between basic or primary emotions and cognitive or secondary emotions. Basic emotions are generally understood to be innate, firmly anchored in human evolutionary biology, having evolved for adaptive functions, and expressed in involuntary reactions to stimuli, including universally recognisable facial expressions.[7] A classic example is Paul Ekman's use of cross-cultural recognition of facial expressions to identify six basic emotions: fear, anger, sadness, disgust, happiness, and surprise.[8] This focus on external responses may in fact have caused some emotions to be overlooked.[9] But even when priority is given to external signals for identifying emotions, the category of basic emotions is not so clear-cut, as we will soon see.

It is of course true that self-conscious emotions, as we normally understand them and carve them up, require a conscious self. But even the basic emotions do

---

[6] Jonathan Haidt, "The Moral Emotions," in *Handbook of Affective Sciences* (ed. Richard J. Davidson, Klaus R. Scherer, and H. Hill Goldsmith; Oxford: Oxford University Press, 2003), 852–870. One may rightly argue that all types of emotions influence moral behaviour. Other-condemning emotions, however, are understood to guard especially against moral transgressions of others.

[7] Sherri C. Widen, "The Development of Children's Concepts of Emotions," in *Handbook of Emotions*, 4th ed. (ed. Lisa Feldman Barrett, Michael Lewis, and Jeanette Haviland-Jones; New York: Guilford, 2016), 307–318 (310–311).

[8] Paul Ekman, "Facial Expression and Emotion," *American Psychologist* 48 (1993): 384–392.

[9] Naomi I. Eisenberger, "Social Pain and Social Pleasure: Two Overlooked but Fundamental Mammalian Emotions," in *Handbook of Emotions*, 4th ed. (ed. Lisa Feldman Barrett, Michael Lewis, and Jeanette Haviland-Jones; New York: Guilford, 2016), 440–452 (446).

at least require "cognition necessary for perception," as Michael Lewis points out.[10] Lewis describes infant development: at the age of 15–18 months, self-aware-ness emerges in the child, but of a non-evaluative kind, which gives rise to "self-conscious exposed emotions," such as envy, empathy, and non-evaluative embar-rassment. Embarrassment is caused by the self being observed. Around the age of three, cognition has evolved to a point where the child can conceptualize rules and goals, which goes together with the emergence of "self-conscious evaluative emo-tions," including evaluative embarrassment, pride, shame, and guilt.[11]

Embarrassment, shame, and guilt are often distinguished from each other, with embarrassment requiring self-attention or self-consciousness, shame signal-ling a threat to the social self, and guilt responding to undesirable behaviour. Shame involves a loss of (self-) esteem and concern for loss of social status, while guilt can be thought of as more active and intent on reparation. Some see embar-rassment as fairly distanced from both shame and guilt, while others regard it as a weak form of shame, in which the core self is not questioned.[12] The latter sugges-tion would fit with Lewis' evaluative embarrassment, but less with his non-evalu-ative embarrassment. Non-evaluative embarrassment, in fact, is more akin to shy-ness, which is less often discussed, and which Rowland Miller finds to be a "*future-oriented* mood state," rather than an emotion.[13] Be that as it may, shyness can be placed at one end of a spectrum in which guilt belongs to the other and embarrass-ment "is a cousin of both shyness and shame but is clearly different from either one."[14]

The fact that self-conscious emotions require a conscious self does not mean that they are less biologically based than the so-called basic emotions. The argu-ment for a secondary status from the lack of global facial expressions is not so strong as one would think. Embarrassment is often accompanied by blushing, alt-hough individual tendencies to blush vary and visibility depends on skin colour.

---

[10] Michael Lewis, "Self-Conscious Emotional Development," in *The Self-Conscious Emo-tions: Theory and Research* (ed. Jessica L. Tracy, Richard W. Robins, and June Price Tangney; New York: Guilford, 2007), 134–149 (134).

[11] Lewis, "Self-Conscious Emotional Development," 134–135.

[12] Tara L. Gruenewald, Sally S. Dickerson, and Margaret E. Kemeny, "A Social Function for Self-Conscious Emotions: The Social Self Preservation Theory," in *The Self-Conscious Emotions: Theory and Research* (ed. Jessica L. Tracy, Richard W. Robins, and June Price Tangney; New York: Guilford, 2007), 68–87 (68–71).

[13] Rowland S. Miller, "Is Embarrassment a Blessing or a Curse?" in *The Self-Conscious Emo-tions: Theory and Research* (ed. Jessica L. Tracy, Richard W. Robins, and June Price Tangney; New York: Guilford, 2007), 245–262 (246).

[14] Miller, "Embarrassment," 246.

The physical reaction is automatic and due to constrictions and expansions of blood vessels. Experiments show that people who blush at mishaps are regarded more sympathetically and judged more leniently than those who do not. The reaction cannot be faked, and it signals sincerity.[15]

Blushing may also accompany shame, although not so frequently, and the role of blushing ascribed by Darwin is partly unwarranted. Moreover, the fluid border between embarrassment and shame complicates our assessment.[16] Shame, embarrassment, and guilt, however, do have certain body signals in common. These revolve around body posture: people lower their face and sometimes tilt their head downward to the side, they avoid looks and slump their shoulders, in a shrivelled-up posture, which is virtually the opposite to displays of pride.[17] Interestingly, these are similar to defensive responses by infants to interpersonal disruptions.[18] There are several arguments for these signals being innate and the results of evolutionary adaptation. First, both pride and shame displays are equally exhibited in response to success and failure, and equally recognized as such in remotely diverse cultures like the industrialised West and in small-scale societies in Burkina Faso and Fiji.[19] Secondly, these behaviours were displayed similarly by sighted, blind, and congenitally blind athletes from more than thirty countries at victory and defeat respectively, in the Paralympics. The only difference was that individuals from Western, highly individualistic cultures, moderated their shame responses, *except* for the congenitally blind, which further underscores that these behaviours tend

---

[15] Miller, "Embarrassment," 251–252. However, the embarrassment displayed needs to correspond to the context; exaggerated reactions have an opposite effect.

[16] Charles Darwin, *The Expression of the Emotions in Man and Animals* (The Works of Charles Darwin 23; New York: New York University Press, 1989 [originally published 1872]), chapter 13; cf. Michael Lewis, "Self-Conscious Emotions: Embarrassment, Pride, Shame, Guilt, and Hubris," in *Handbook of Emotions*, 4th ed. (ed. Lisa Feldman Barrett, Michael Lewis, and Jeanette Haviland-Jones; New York: Guilford, 2016), 792–814 (793–795).

[17] Gruenewald, Dickerson, and Kemeny, "A Social Function," 73.

[18] Paul Gilbert, "The Evolution of Shame as a Marker for Relationship Security: A Biopsychosocial Approach," in *The Self-Conscious Emotions: Theory and Research* (ed. Jessica L. Tracy, Richard W. Robins, and June Price Tangney; New York: Guilford, 2007), 283–309 (291).

[19] Dacher Keltner *et al.*, "Expression of Emotion," in *Handbook of Emotions*, 4th ed. (ed. Lisa Feldman Barrett, Michael Lewis, and Jeanette Haviland-Jones; New York: Guilford, 2016), 467–482 (470).

to be innate.[20] Thirdly, these displays are similar to dominance and submission be-haviours among other animals, studied by researchers.[21]

The last point of course raises the question of the evolutionary roots of the shame family of emotions. On the one hand, shame requires certain cognitive ca-pacities necessary for self-consciousness and self-evaluation. These requirements basically correspond to what evolutionary theorists call "theory of mind," the ca-pacity to understand other individuals to the extent that one can see oneself through their eyes, that is, simulate how others evaluate and appraise one's own behaviour.[22] This makes for an *inner* inner world,[23] something human beings share to at least some extent with other intelligent social species, such as higher primates, elephants, and dolphins. On the other hand, shame (or embarrassment) displays apparently have an innate, biological substratum behind, or independent of, conscious behaviour. Although bodily reactions can be partially controlled, this is difficult, and public shame displays hardly enhance status, but openly de-clare failure. In spite of this, they are adaptive, if shame is understood within the framework of a social hierarchy as a sign of submission to those in power and of loyalty to the group.[24]

We usually associate shame with the public failure to comply with some cul-tural or moral standards for behaviour, meaning that we know that others are aware of our failure. When shame is studied cross-culturally, however, it becomes evident that there need not be any failure to comply with social or moral rules, but the mere encounter with superiors or people of higher status is sufficient to trigger

---

[20] Jessica L. Tracy and David Matsumoto, "The Spontaneous Expression of Pride and Shame: Evidence for Biologically Innate Nonverbal Displays," *Proceedings of the National Acad-emy of Sciences* 105 (2008): 11655–11660.

[21] Gruenewald, Dickerson, and Kemeny, "A Social Function," 73.

[22] For a short overview with research history and a discussion of the evolutionary origins of theory of mind, see Ioannis Tsoukalas, "Theory of Mind: Towards an Evolutionary Theory," *Evolutionary Psychological Science* 4 (2018): 38–66. For now classic studies, see David Premack and Guy Woodruff, "Does the Chimpanzee Have a Theory of Mind?" *The Behavioral and Brain Sciences* 4 (1978): 515–526; Alan M. Leslie, "Pretense and Representation: The Origins of 'Theory of Mind'," *Psychological Review* 94 (1987): 412–426.

[23] For this expression, see Peter Gärdenfors, *How Homo Became Sapiens: On the Evolution of Thinking* (Oxford: Oxford University Press, 2006), 111–140.

[24] Dacher Keltner and LeeAnne Harker, "The Forms and Functions of the Nonverbal Sig-nals of Shame," in *Shame: Interpersonal Behavior, Psychopathology, and Culture* (ed. Paul Gilbert and Bernice Andrews; New York: Oxford University Press, 1998), 78–98; Gruenewald, Dicker-son, and Kemeny, "A Social Function"; Elizabeth Jacqueline Dansie, "An Empirical Investiga-tion of the Adaptive Nature of Shame" (M.Sc. diss., Utah State University, 2009).

shame. Daniel Fessler talks of this as "subordinance shame."[25] Such shame, says Fessler

> is evolutionarily ancient [and] is bolstered by the fact that recognizing that one occupies an inferior position in a social hierarchy requires far less cognitive complexity than does recognizing that others know that one has failed. ... It is ... likely that the common ancestor of humans and primates likewise lacked the cognitive capacity for a theory of mind, and hence that any emotions experienced by this species were not dependent on this capacity, making it all the more plausible that subordinance shame is the original or primordial aspect of this emotion.[26]

Fessler suggests that for nonhuman primates, lacking cultural criteria to measure success, social position was a function of dominance, but human societies developed prestige hierarchies in which dominant positions were given rather than taken.[27] The history of humankind suggests that both models coexist, and that culture is perhaps a thin veneer. But the theory makes sense of shame behaviours as originally appeasement displays, which signalled submission rather than fight, and helped losers avoid injury or death. On the other hand, they lost in status. The reason for shame displays still being part of the human involuntary repertoire is probably that they communicate submission, cooperation, loyalty to superiors, and willingness to follow group norms. In the long run, there was more to gain by cooperation and coordination. By displaying submissive or subordinance shame, one could perhaps partner with the winners instead of being killed by them.[28] Self-conscious emotions facilitated and regulated both group cooperation and group organisation.[29]

Shame in Continuum

In human groups, innate and biologically based capacities are largely formed by culture and cultural diversity leads to a variety of expressions. This becomes visible

---

[25] Daniel M. T. Fessler, "From Appeasement to Conformity: Evolutionary and Cultural Perspectives on Shame, Competition, and Cooperation," in *The Self-Conscious Emotions: Theory and Research* (ed. Jessica L. Tracy, Richard W. Robins, and June Price Tangney; New York: Guilford, 2007), 174–193 (175–176).

[26] Fessler, "From Appeasement to Conformity," 176.

[27] Fessler, "From Appeasement to Conformity," 176.

[28] Fessler, "From Appeasement to Conformity," 177–182.

[29] Jennifer L. Goetz and Dacher Keltner, "Shifting Meanings of Self-Conscious Emotions Across Cultures: A Social-Functional Approach," in *The Self-Conscious Emotions: Theory and Research* (ed. Jessica L. Tracy, Richard W. Robins, and June Price Tangney; New York: Guilford, 2007), 153–173 (154–156).

not least in language. Historical and contextual factors shape the ways in which emotions are expressed by actions as well as by words and harness emotions in the service of cultural ideals and practices. Embarrassment, guilt, and shame concepts are not identical between cultures, but overlap in various ways. The meaning of shame varies considerably depending on whether it expresses failure to uphold norms of reciprocity or norms of hierarchy.[30] Emotions are valued differently in different cultures. Western, individualistic cultures have little patience with shame and more or less ignore subordinance shame, even though they have the capacity to understand it. Many non-Western cultures, on the other hand, regard subordinance, shyness, and respect as shame's core, while guilt is less prominent, or even lacking.[31] To note this is not the same as affirming the old dichotomy between shame cultures and guilt cultures, which is far too simplified.

Emotion words in one language lose nuances and take on partly new meanings when translated. In a cross-cultural study, Robin Edelstein and Phillip Shaver demonstrate that shame words in a specific language can be identified as part of particular emotion clusters, but these clusters vary. In English and Italian, shame and guilt are clustered together within the sadness cluster. In Indonesian and Dutch, however, shame and embarrassment fall into the fear cluster (but not guilt in Indonesian). In certain languages, shame is not even distinguished from fear. These examples may suffice to prove that differences depend on cultural contexts, as whether shame is associated primarily with anxiety or regret. Also, some languages use separate concepts for emotions which in other languages are identified by one word and only regarded as degrees of intensity.[32]

Based on all of the considerations discussed so far, I shall propose a scheme of emotions belonging to the shame family along a continuum, in order to differentiate as far as possible between various nuances and aspects. I should strongly emphasize that I do this entirely for heuristic purposes. The ways in which we carve up the field of self-conscious emotions is, although based on biopsychosocial considerations, still in many ways arbitrary, or at least highly culture-specific and contextual. I do this, however, to get a handle on shame and shame-related texts from the Bible.

---

[30] Cf. Goetz and Keltner, "Shifting Meanings," 168.

[31] Fessler, "From Appeasement to Conformity," 184–185.

[32] Robin S. Edelstein and Phillip R. Shaver, "A Cross-Cultural Examination of Lexical Studies of Self-Conscious Emotions," in *The Self-Conscious Emotions: Theory and Research* (ed. Jessica L. Tracy, Richard W. Robins, and June Price Tangney; New York: Guilford, 2007), 194–208 (198–199).

	SHYNESS I	SHYNESS II / EMBARRASSMENT I	EMBARRASSMENT II / SHAME I	SHAME II (FEAR?)	SHAME III / GUILT I	GUILT II
Character	Future-oriented mood Long-term Non-event	Non-evaluative social attention Event	Negative social evaluation *Subordinance shame*	Negative social evaluation and self-evaluation, *Subordinance shame*	Negative social evaluation and self-evaluation	Negative social evaluation and self-evaluation Moral responsibility
Problem	Uncomfortable with self-awareness	Uncomfortable with others' observation	Judgment Lack of status	Undesirable self Loss of status and control Failure	Undesirable action Loss of integrity	Undesirable action Loss of integrity Loss of self-respect
Body Reaction	Hide Look away	Hide Blush Look away Nervous touching	Sheepish smile Blush Look away Lower face, tilt head, slump shoulders etc.	Blush or pale? Look away Lower face, tilt head, slump shoulders etc.	Blush or pale? Look away Lower face, tilt head, slump shoulders etc.	Look away Lower face, tilt head, slump shoulders etc.
Signal	I don't want to be here	I am interested, but nervous	I want to be accepted I adapt	I accept my place I submit I appease I am no threat I am not faking	I accept norms I show respect I am not faking	I make reparation I reform I subscribe to norms I am not faking Display loyalty
Function	Avoidance	Divert attention	Receive empathy	Survival Avoid punishment	Resume cooperation	Resume trustworthiness

The point of this scheme is *not* to nail characteristics or reactions to a particular "phase," but to illustrate the overlaps and fuzzy borders between various self-conscious emotional categories. Many details are indeed open to question and in several instances, one could discuss whether items belong here or there or under several columns. The visual column structure itself in a way counteracts or contradicts the message about the shame family emotions along a continuum.

The two types of embarrassment, which were already previously mentioned, overlap with shyness as well as with shame, and shame and guilt are not clearly separable. Different cultures and languages construct different categories along this continuum and there are no hard and fast rules. In some cases, even certain types of shyness and shame may be subsumed under the same concept, as we will see with the Greek αἰδώς.

The most conspicuous observation is perhaps that SHAME II, which I have marked in bold above, has very little, if anything at all, to do with norm transgression or morality, but entirely with failure and loss of status. There is no wrongdoing behind such shame, but plain failure to stay in control and defend one's honour or privileged position visavi competitors or enemies. Loss of control in this sense might incur real danger, which makes concomitant body reactions related to fear just as predictable as those related to embarrassment. The fact that some languages relate shame vocabulary to the fear cluster gives support to such an explanation and to an explicit association of SHAME II with FEAR, as indicated in the scheme above. An example of this is the Hebrew בוש, which is occasionally associated with a pale face, as we will see examples of.

SHAME II corresponds largely to what Fessler calls subordinance shame, although some important characteristics of subordinance shame are also displayed in EMBARRASSMENT II/ SHAME I. It is marked in italics in the scheme above. From an evolutionary point of view, subordinance shame, especially as represented in SHAME II, reflects a prototypical or ancient type of shame. Body reactions and signals have evolved to ensure survival within a hierarchical structure, in a way analogous to how many social animal species behave. The character of negative evaluation is in a way secondary to, or dependent on, the fact that one has been forced to hand over power and/or status to others, or somehow lost control regardless of any specific norm-breaking behaviour. One could discuss whether SHAME II or subordinance shame should be regarded as paradigmatic for the shame family, or rather as an archaic, underlying substratum, or perhaps as both. As we will see, it accounts for no small part of the textual examples we now turn to.

Shame in the Hebrew Bible

The primary term for shame in the Hebrew Bible is the root בּוֹשׁ. The verb is found more than 130 times and there are a few instances of the two nouns, בּוּשָׁה and בֹּשֶׁת.[33] בּוֹשׁ is generally translated into Greek with αἰσχύνειν, occasionally with καταισχύνειν, in the LXX. It is often used in the Psalms and in the major prophets Isaiah and Jeremiah, with a few other references scattered in other books. It is fairly often paralleled with חפר, כְּלִמָּה/כלם, and חֶרְפָּה (the latter root is mostly represented by ὀνειδίζειν, while the two former are normally rendered by ἐντρέπειν in the LXX). The cluster of meanings focus on humiliation, insult, and infringement.[34]

The three roots, בּוֹשׁ, כלם, and חפר, are carefully analysed in Martin Klopfenstein's classic "concept-historical" (*begriffsgeschichtliche*) study on shame in the Hebrew Bible from 1972.[35] Klopfenstein argues that shame and guilt are intrinsically (*von Haus aus*) associated, shame being the subjective expression of feeling guilt and shaming being the objective expression of exposed guilt.[36] The near equation of shame with guilt has been criticised among others by Lyn Bechtel Huber, who demonstrates how both formal (judicial and political) and informal (social) shaming function as sanctions of behaviour for a number of contexts in which sanctions involving guilt would not have been appropriate, and that shaming would often have been more powerful, due to the group-oriented character of society.[37]

Separating guilt from shame is admittedly more easily said than done, as already indicated in the preceding section, and Johanna Stiebert, who has written another monograph on Shame in the Hebrew Bible, commends Klopfenstein for

---

[33] There is also the less common מְבוּשִׁים and בָּשְׁנָה. בֹּשֶׁת is conspicuously used as a dysphemism for various "foreign" gods, in particular Baal, by replacing the theophoric element in names such as Ish-Baal (> Ish-Boshet), and by its vowels replacing the original ones in divine names such as Ashtart (> Ashtoreth) and perhaps Molech. Marvin H. Pope, "Bible, Euphemism and Dysphemism in the," *ABD* 1:720–725.

[34] Alexandra Grund-Wittenberg, "Scham / Schande (AT)," 2015, in *Das wissenschaftliche Bibellexikon im Internet (WiBiLex)*, http://www.bibelwissenschaft.de/stichwort/26305/; Horst Seebass, "בּוֹשׁ *bôsh*; בּוּשָׁה *bûshāh*; בֹּשֶׁת *bôsheth*; מְבוּשִׁים *mᵉbûshîm*," *TDOT*, vol. 2, rev. ed. (ed. G. Johannes Botterweck and Helmer Ringgren; Grand Rapids, MI: Eerdmans, 1977), 50–60.

[35] Martin Klopfenstein, *Scham und Schande nach dem Alten Testament: eine begriffsgeschichtliche Untersuchung zu den hebräischen Wurzeln bôš, klm und ḥpr* (ATANT 62; Zürich: Theologischer Verlag, 1972).

[36] Klopfenstein, *Scham und Schande*, 33, 49.

[37] Lyn M. Bechtel, "Shame as Sanction of Social Control in Biblical Israel: Judicial, Political, and Social Shaming," *Journal for the Study of the Old Testament* 49: 47–76.

keeping shame and guilt together. She is, however, critical of his understanding of how בוש-language developed from its purported first use in the sexual domain in Hosea.[38] Stiebert's own monograph takes inspiration from psychological research and focuses on the three major prophets Isaiah, Jeremiah, and Ezekiel. She attempts to prove the insufficiency of the honour-shame paradigm from Mediterranean studies for studying shame in the Hebrew Bible.[39]

In spite of Klopfenstein's detailed analyses, there are some major weaknesses. His view of בוש finding its origins in the sexual sphere (Gen 2:25; Hos 2:7) depends at least partly (for Genesis) on outdated or highly questionable source theories; his close association of בוש with cultic issues is arguably a result of over-interpretation; and his fundamental distinction between secular and theological usages of shame-terminology is strained and results from a certain theological bias.[40]

Many scholars point out that shame in the Hebrew Bible is mainly about loss of status and has little to do with an inner experience or introvert feeling but is associated with rather physical aspects.[41] Shame can result from one's own failure, or from being let down by significant others, as when Joab complains about David's behaviour against those who have saved him (2 Sam 19:6). Yael Avrahami suggests that the meaning of the root בוש is often "disappointment" or "failure," rather than shame in our sense. In her investigation of בוש-language in the Psalms, she demonstrates that such translations work well. The synonyms that בוש is juxtaposed to, belong to the semantic field of worthlessness and suggest that בוש is a negative experience. Only some of the synonyms are shame words. Moreover, none of the antonyms that appear is an honour word, but they all refer to positive experiences: to save, to be happy, to be satisfied.[42] Avrahami suggests that בוש "has to do with the experience of a disconnection between expectations and reality"[43] and she concludes with a few additional examples from the prophets. She suggests that the idea of two or three homonymic roots (בוש I, II, and III) is quite un-

---

[38] Johanna Stiebert, *The Construction of Shame in the Hebrew Bible: The Prophetic Contribution* (JSOTSup 346; Sheffield: Sheffield Academic Press, 2002), 44–50.

[39] Stiebert, *Construction of Shame*, 165–173.

[40] Klopfenstein, *Scham und Schande*, 31–33, 58–60; for the secular-theological distinction, see the whole structure of Klopfenstein's work.

[41] Margaret S. Odell, "The Inversion of Shame and Forgiveness in Ezekiel 16.59–63," *Journal for the Study of the Old Testament* 56 (1992): 101–112 (103); Matthew J. Lynch, "Neglected Physical Dimensions of 'Shame'," *Biblica* 91 (2010): 499–517, who suggests physical experiences of diminishment or harm.

[42] Avrahami, "בוש in the Psalms."

[43] Avrahami, "בוש in the Psalms," 308.

necessary and that texts in which a homonymic root has been supposed would also receive a simpler and more plausible interpretation, assuming a single root and taking her suggestions into account.[44] To spell this out: Moses *failed* to come down from the mountain (Exod 32:1), Sisera's mother asks "why does his chariot *fail* to return?" (Judg 5:24), Ezra says that he *failed* to ask for soldiers (Ezra 8:22), and the expression עד־בּוֹשׁ simply means "to the point of despair."

Avrahami's suggestion fits well with SHAME II in our scheme, which has a focus on failure and loss of control. For example, Psalm 35 is framed by a prayer to YHWH for the failure of the author's opponents.

v. 4 יֵבֹשׁוּ וְיִכָּלְמוּ מְבַקְשֵׁי נַפְשִׁי יִסֹּגוּ אָחוֹר וְיַחְפְּרוּ חֹשְׁבֵי רָעָתִי:

Let them be ashamed and humiliated who seek my life. May they be turned back and embarrassed who plan my evil.

v. 26 יֵבֹשׁוּ וְיַחְפְּרוּ יַחְדָּו שְׂמֵחֵי רָעָתִי יִלְבְּשׁוּ־בֹשֶׁת וּכְלִמָּה הַמַּגְדִּילִים עָלָי:

Let them be ashamed and embarrassed together who rejoiced over my distress. May they be clothed with shame and reproach who magnify themselves over me.

The author hopes that those who seek his life, those who rejoice over his distress, will be shamed, covered with shame, meaning that he wishes them to be disappointed, unsuccessful, and fail in their intention. Here is a case of possible loss of status and control, perhaps a matter of survival. Shame can be similarly interpreted in Isa 54:5, where it is explicitly associated with widowhood, i.e., being let down without support, and in Jer 20:11, where בוש is juxtaposed to failure (stumbling; כשל ni.). And in Isa 24:23 the sun and the moon are shamed before YHWH, meaning that they submit to his authority: a clear example of subordinance shame.

In 2 Kings 19:26, Isaiah says about Sennacherib's destruction of cities: וְיֹשְׁבֵיהֶן קִצְרֵי־יָד חַתּוּ וַיֵּבֹשׁוּ (their inhabitants are powerless, terrified, and shamed). The "shame" is here juxtaposed to fear and concerns mere survival, it has little to do with norm infringement or loss of integrity. The association with fear makes sense of Isa 29:22, in which shame is paralleled to faces growing pale or white.

לֹא־עַתָּה יֵבוֹשׁ יַעֲקֹב וְלֹא עַתָּה פָּנָיו יֶחֱוָרוּ

Jacob will no longer be shamed, and his face will no longer grow pale.

The verb חור can hardly be translated as "blushing," as is occasionally done. This is not the reddening of embarrassment, but a sign of fear, a paling associated with subordinance shame.

---

[44] Avrahami, "בוש in the Psalms," 310–313.

This does not mean that בוש and other shame vocabulary are *only* used in contexts of what I call SHAME II, but meanings like failure, disappointment, or being let down, go a long way, even taking figures like being "wrapped in shame" or "shame covers my head" into regard. There are instances, however, which go beyond a SHAME II framework, even though Isaiah's idol worshippers may probably pass for failures (e.g., Isa 42:17; 44:9, 11; 45:16, 17; cf. Ps 97:7) and Jeremiah's oracles against the nations being put to shame, too (e.g., Egypt 46:24; Moab 48:39; Damascus 49:23; Bel and his idols 50:2; Babylon 50:12; 51:47). In Ezekiel shame is clearly associated with sexual misconduct (16:52, 63) and explicitly associated with sinful and abominable behaviour (36:31–32).[45] The framework for shame here is clearly SHAME III/ GUILT I. Although the shame of nakedness (or rather, lack of shame) in the garden of Eden narrative (Gen 2:25) might possibly be understood as "they suffered no harm," this is contrived. It seems reasonable to read this text within the framework of EMBARRASSMENT II/ SHAME I: there is no negative social evaluation or lack of acceptance, in spite of the fact that the man and the woman are unclothed. The meaning of shame does move along a continuum, but subordinance shame and failure have the capacity to account for more than we might have thought and there is little need for overly theological explanations.

Shame in Greek, in the LXX, and in Ben Sira

The translation of the Hebrew Bible into Greek introduces terminology with different connotations and overlaps. The main Greek terms revolve around two stems, αἰδ- and αἰσχ-. Douglas Cairns' major study on αἰδώς in Homer and classical literature lays the groundwork for all subsequent discussion.[46] Cairns also discusses αἰσχύνη, αἰσχρός and other relevant terms. For our purpose, similarities and differences between αἰδ- and αἰσχ-terms are of most interest.

From Homer and onwards, αἰδώς and αἰδεῖσθαι describe a sense of propriety and respect, an emotion of bashfulness, embarrassment, or inhibition, especially before people of higher status or with more power. Basically, the vocabulary suggests "shame" of a sort that belongs within the frameworks of SHYNESS II/ EMBARRASSMENT I and EMBARRASSMENT II/ SHAME I. Cairns states that αἰδώς cannot be equated with shame precisely because it covers both shame and embarrass-

---

[45] The attempt by Odell ("Inversion of Shame") to explain the mouth opening in Ezek 16:63 does not change this fact.

[46] Douglas L. Cairns, AIDŌS: *The Psychology and Ethics on Honour and Shame in Ancient Greek Literature* (Oxford: Clarendon, 1993).

ment.[47] To feel and express αἰδώς is then, in a slightly paradoxical way, equal to showing honour to those stronger or of more status than you. In that sense, it is typical of subordinance shame, although not *necessarily* associated with *loss* of status and control, but often just representing the appropriate behaviour towards someone with a higher position on the hierarchical ladder, for whatever reason.

The example of Nausikaa, from the Odyssey's sixth song, is a classic one, which also indicates the extent to which αἰδώς was a particularly female virtue; at least it induced certain behaviours for women and partly others for men. In spite of her initiative and endeavour for liberty, Nausikaa displays deference and restraint, she is modest as befits women in Greek archaic and classical culture.

The gendered aspects of αἰδώς / αἰδεῖσθαι are elaborated by the tragedist Euripides (5th century BCE) in *Ifigenia in Aulis* 558–72, a passage in which the chorus clearly delineates the role of shame as modesty within the context of the current hierarchical social order:

> διάφοροι δὲ φύσεις βροτῶν, διάφοροι δὲ τρόποι· τὸ δ' ὀρθῶς ἐσθλὸν σαφὲς αἰεί· τροφαί θ' αἱ παιδευόμεναι μέγα φέρουσ' ἐς τὰν ἀρετάν· τό τε γὰρ **αἰδεῖσθαι** σοφία, τάν τ'ἐξαλλάσσουσαν ἔχει χάριν ὑπὸ γνώμας ἐσορᾶν τὸ δέον, ἔνθα δόξα φέρει κλέος ἀγήρατον βιοτᾷ. μέγα τι θηρεύειν ἀρετάν, **γυναιξὶ μὲν** κατὰ Κύπριν **κρυπτάν**, ἐν **ἀνδράσι** δ' αὖ **κόσμος** ἐνὼν ὁ μυριοπληθὴς μείζω πόλιν αὔξει.

> The natures of mortals vary, and their habits differ, but the truly good is always plain: educated upbringings greatly lead to virtue; for **modesty** is wisdom and has the extraordinary gift to judiciously discern what is fitting. Then reputation brings ageless renown to life. Great it is to hunt for virtue, **for women** according to the **covert** Kypris [i.e., a discrete gender role], while **for men**, the infinite and innate [sense of] **order** makes a city grow big.

In contrast to αἰδώς, αἰσχρός basically means "ugly" in opposition to καλός and although αἰσχύνη is generally "shame," or "disgrace," the active αἰσχύνειν is to disfigure. To be ashamed (αἰσχύνεσθαι, ἐπαισχύνεσθαι), or to shame (καταισχύνειν), are basically aesthetic terms, applied also, but not exclusively within moral frameworks.

In his study on shame and necessity in ancient Greece, Bernard Williams explains that he does not separate uses of the two roots αἰδ- and αἰσχύν-, because he finds variations to be mainly diachronic, so that αἰσχύνη (shame) increasingly took the place of αἰδώς (respect).[48] Rudolf Bultmann had already pointed out that

---

[47] Cairns, AIDŌS, 7.
[48] Bernard Williams, *Shame and Necessity* (Berkeley, CA: University of California Press, 1993), 194, n.9.

although αἰδεῖσθαι was always in use, αἰδώς "became rare in the time of Hellenism, but was brought back into use by the late Stoics."[49]

The fact that αἰσχύνεσθαι can be found as an equivalent to αἰδώς already in Homer and that αἰδώς / αἰδεῖσθαι continued in use with two senses as well gives David Konstan reason to protest against a simplified chronological argument.[50] In any case, Homer only has three occurrences of αἰσχύνεσθαι, all in the *Odyssey*, and Cairns concludes, after having discussed them one by one, that Homer's passages should not be use as "evidence for any fundamental difference in the function and significance of the two verbs."[51] Nevertheless, says Konstan, there is a slight difference in that αἰδώς normally has a prospective or inhibitory sense, while αἰσχύνη also can reflect back on disapproved behaviour with regret – something that Konstan demonstrates from Aristotle's *Nicomachean Ethics*.[52] To what extent such a differentiation is relevant to more general usage is debatable; Bultmann suggests that this is a Stoic distinction that does not really correspond to actual usage, and that both terms can be used in a prospective as well as a reflective sense.[53]

In relation to our heuristic scheme, we might suggest that αἰσχ- terminology perhaps fits best within the frameworks of SHAME III/GUILT I and GUILT II, but can also be used in the framework of EMBARRASSMENT II/SHAME I. This reminds us again, first that the scheme is heuristic and not meant to draw borders but to point to overlaps within a continuum, and secondly that an underlying stratum of subordinance shame often makes itself known all along the continuum.

When the Hebrew Bible is translated into Greek, בוש is usually translated with αἰσχύνη and αἰσχύνεσθαι. This introduces connotations of social and moral norms that were not unknown to בוש, but fairly marginal, at least not dominant. It is not difficult to imagine the effect when the struggle for status and control, reflected in Ps 35, is read through the lens of Greek expressions for shame and shaming. The fearful shame easily becomes moralised if fear is understood to mean fear of punishment for bad behaviour and faces and heads covered with shame are possible to interpret as blushing and strong feelings of remorse, the effects of which we can see above all in modern translations.

---

[49] Rudolf Bultmann, "αἰδώς," in *TDNT*, vol. 1 (ed. Gerhard Kittel; Grand Rapids, MI: Eerdmans, 1964), 169–171 (169).

[50] Konstan, *Emotions*, 93–94.

[51] Cairns, AIDŌS, 138–139.

[52] Konstan, *Emotions*, 94–96; the example he quotes is from *Eth. Nic.* 1128b.

[53] Bultmann, "αἰδώς," 170.

Ben Sira provides a window into this cultural blending process since his writing is packed with shame and some of his passages on shame are extant in both Hebrew and Greek. After having admonished his son not to be ashamed of himself (ואל נפשך אל תבוש) / περὶ τῆς ψυχῆς σου μὴ αἰσχυνθῇς), Ben Sira distinguishes between two types of shame, or embarrassment in 4:21:

כי יש בֹּשֶׁת מַשׂאת עון ויש בשת כבוד וחן:[54]

ἔστιν γὰρ αἰσχύνη ἐπάγουσα ἁμαρτίαν καὶ ἔστιν αἰσχύνη δόξα καὶ χάρις

For there is a shame leading to sin, and there is a shame to glory and favour.

The Hebrew text uses בוש here in a sense already influenced by Greek conceptualisation and the term is consequently translated with αἰσχύνη. If we were to claim a clear distinction between different terms in Greek shame vocabulary, the second instance of בוש would rather be represented by αἰδώς, but this is not the case, as αἰσχύνη also takes on the meaning of "sense of shame." αἰσχύνη can obviously be used along the whole continuum, from embarrassment to guilt. The shame that leads to sin would most probably refer to disapproved behaviour,[55] but the shame that leads to honour and praise could refer not only to inhibitory shame, preventing misdeeds, but also to subordinance shame, resulting in appropriate behaviour towards superiors and seniors in a hierarchical society. This is at least what Ben Sira recommends in the beginning of chapter 4: μεγιστᾶνι ταπείνου τὴν κεφαλήν σου – lower your head before the mighty (4:7b).

In 41:14–42:8, Ben Sira provides lists of behaviours of which one should and should not be ashamed of. One *should* be ashamed (בוש/ αἰσχύνεσθε) of adultery, lies, and a number of named crimes, but also of placing one's elbow in the food. Sex and money figure repeatedly, as we would expect. One should *not* be ashamed of the law, so as to be partial and acquit the ungodly, nor of keeping accounts, making a profit, disciplining one's children, or maltreating one's slave. Of the

---

[54] Manuscript A1 Verso. See https://www.bensira.org/ for facsimile and Martin Abegg's transcription. Manuscript C1 Verso has חן וכבוד, i.e., the opposite order.

[55] We would perhaps expect the reverse, that sin leads to shame, but the Greek meaning is probably that shame (αἰσχύνη) in the sense of shameful *behaviour* leads (ἐπάγουσα) to sin. On the other hand, the Greek formulation may be the result of struggling with the Hebrew *Vorlage*: the translator seems to have taken משאת as a verbal noun derived from נשא and hence a raising or carrying, which has been interpreted in Greek as leading to, or bringing (out) sin. Based on the same root the Hebrew could also be taken to mean that shame is an offering to sin, a burden of sin, or even a signal or sign of sin (cf. the use of מַשְׂאָ for beacon, fire-signal; Judg 20:38; Jer 6:1). There is an additional possibility: מִשֹּׁאַת (מֵן + שׁוֹאָה cstr, as in Prov 3:25), which would render the meaning "there is a shame from the disaster of sin."

behaviours in the first list, Ben Sira says, "you may be legitimately ashamed (והיית
בושׁ באמת / ἔσῃ αἰσχυντηρὸς ἀληθινῶς) and find grace in all people's eyes" (Sir 42:1;
LXX 41:27). This is a shame which looks forward and makes a person anticipate
the detrimental results of acting against the norms so as to avoid such actions. One
could possibly sense a difference in nuance here between the Hebrew and the
Greek: the Hebrew may be interpreted as "you will be truly embarrassed for such
behaviour (and thus avoid it)," while the Greek could perhaps be taken to mean
"if you show the right shame and avoid such behaviour, you will become truly
'shameful', in the sense of a 'modest person'."[56] In any case, the shame vocabulary
employed here, in Hebrew as well as in Greek, stretches over the frameworks of at
least SHAME I, II, and III. The fundamentally hierarchic character of the emotion
of shame is not affected, but the process through which Israel is becoming embedded in Hellenistic culture seems to have shifted the emphasis of shame also in Hebrew, at least in Ben Sira, towards the moralistic side.[57]

Shame in the New Testament

If we expect to see a continuation of such a "moral turn" in the New Testament
writings, we may be disappointed. Space does not allow for more than a cursory
overview of the most relevant material, but this is hopefully enough to discern a
general picture.

Only once in the New Testament do we find αἰδώς being used. The term is
paired with σωφροσύνη in a highly patriarchal attempt to regulate women's dress
(1 Tim 2:9–10), followed by detailed instructions about their submission (1 Tim

---

[56] For somewhat related examples of possible differences in nuance between Ben Sira's Hebrew text in a Second Temple Jewish context and the Greek translation in a Hellenistic diaspora
community, see Giuseppe Bellia, "An Historico-Anthropological Reading of the Work of Ben
Sira," in *The Wisdom of Ben Sira: Studies on Tradition, Redaction, and Theology* (ed. Angelo
Passaro and Giuseppe Bellia; Berlin: de Gruyter, 2008), 49–74 (67–68).

[57] The extent of Hellenistic influences in Ben Sira has been subject to much discussion
through the past decades. Ben Sira can be seen to display signs of resistance against the ongoing
Hellenising process, but also to reflect Hellenistic ideology, philosophy, and education, at least
to some extent. For overviews, also discussing previous research, see Oda Wischmeyer, "Die Kon-
struktion von Kultur im Sirachbuch," in *Texts and Contexts of the Book of Sirach / Texte und
Kontexte des Sirachbuches* (ed. Gerhard Karner, Frank Ueberschaer, and Bukard M. Zapff; Sep-
tuagint and Cognate Studies 66; Atlanta, GA: SBL Press, 2017), 71–98; John J. Collins, *Jewish
Wisdom in the Hellenistic Age* (OTL; Louisville, KY: WJK, 1997), especially chapter 2: "Ben Sira
in His Hellenistic Context," 23–41; Patrick W. Skehan and Alexander A. Di Lella, *The Wisdom
of Ben Sira* (AB 39; New York: Doubleday, 1987), 46–50.

2:11–15): women should be shy, embarrassed, or have a sense of shame sufficient to avoid calling attention to themselves, and in particular to avoid speaking in public. This corresponds fairly well with the meaning of αἰδῶς in early Greek usage and is a clear example of subordinance shame. The corresponding verb, αἰδεῖσθαι, is not found in the New Testament at all.[58]

Elsewhere in the New Testament, shame terminology is dominated by the αἰσχ-family (αἰσχρός, αἰσχύνη, αἰσχύνειν, αἰσχύνεσθαι, ἐπαισχύνεσθαι, καταισχύνειν, and a few rare compounds). The scope of this terminology is fairly broad, but can be focused around a few nodes, one of which is gender roles. For example, Paul assumes that everyone finds it αἰσχρός for women to cut their hair (εἰ δὲ αἰσχρὸν γυναικὶ τὸ κείρασθαι ἢ ξυρᾶσθαι; 1 Cor 11:6). Does this mean that Paul found short-haired women ugly? Perhaps not, since the statement is part of an argument that a woman who prays without a head-covering shames her head (καταισχύνει τὴν κεφαλὴν αὐτῆς; 1 Cor 11:5) – an argument to which we will soon return. On the other hand, we might suspect that these aspects were not necessarily or fully kept apart, if we suppose that an aesthetic notion adhered to the concepts of shame that Greek speakers used for thinking and feeling. Another example is the Pauline interpolator (as I take him to be)[59] of 1 Cor 14:35 who, similarly to the author of 1 Tim 2, finds it αἰσχρός for women to speak at public meetings (αἰσχρὸν γάρ ἐστιν γυναικὶ λαλεῖν ἐν ἐκκλησία). These examples reflect a subordinance shame perhaps as much of the EMBARRASSMENT II/SHAME I type as of the SHAME II type. It signals submission and acceptance, even though the problem is lack rather than loss of status.

What about other norm infringements or "moral" issues? It may come as a surprise that such matters are far from the main focus of shame. In addition to texts dealing with gender roles, there are few which explicitly associate shame with immoral behaviour. Paul does it, in Rom 6:21, when he rhetorically asks his addressees what payback ("fruit") they received (τίνα οὖν καρπὸν εἴχετε) when they were slaves under sin, and himself answers: such things you are now ashamed of (ἐφ' οἷς νῦν ἐπαισχύνεσθε), which lead to death. Although the shameful rewards are not explicitly spelled out, it is a fair guess, based on chapter 1, that Paul at least in part has

---

[58] The exception being the variant reading of Heb 12:28, found in the ninth century manuscripts K and L, also attested by a twelwth century corrector (א²) to Codex Sinaiticus.

[59] The literature on 1 Cor 14:34–35 is vast. Gordon Fee's arguments from mainly content and language are by now classic (Gordon D. Fee, *The First Epistle to the Corinthians* [NICNT; Grand Rapids, MI: Eerdmans, 1987], 699–708), and the text-critical argument has been reinforced recently by Philip Payne's study of the distigme-obelos symbols in Codex Vaticanus (Philip B. Payne, "Vaticanus Distigme-obelos Symbols Marking Added Text, Including 1 Corinthians 14.34-5," *New Testament Studies* 63 [2017]: 604–625).

sins of a sexual nature in mind. The author of Eph 5:12 finds it αἰσχρός to speak of what people do in secret (τὰ γὰρ κρυφῇ γινόμενα ὑπ' αὐτῶν αἰσχρόν ἐστιν καὶ λέγειν).[60] We could just imagine what the topic of such conversations might be – in the *Dialogues of the Courtesans*, Lucian lets Leaina express herself similarly, when Clonarion asks for details about how Megilla seduced her: don't ask me for details, they are shameful (αἰσχρά).[61] Jude denounces his opponents (Jude 1:13) by among other things accusing them for "foaming their shames" (ἐπαφρίζοντα τὰς ἑαυτῶν αἰσχύνας), which in the context likely refers to some kind of sexual licentiousness. In a few instances, αἰσχύνη functions as a euphemism for genitals (Phil 3:19; Rev 3:18).[62] Sexual norm infringements are clearly subject to feelings of shame, although it is not evident where on a scale such shame should be placed. One could argue that somewhere within the GUILT spectrum makes sense, but neither loss of integrity, nor a negative self-evaluation is a completely necessary company to the shame involved. In addition to these examples there is surprisingly little evidence in the New Testament for shame language and moral discourse being associated or juxtaposed.[63]

The truth is that much of the shame language in the New Testament relates, just as בּוֹשׁ in the Hebrew Bible, to failure and success. Beginning with Paul, he employs a LXX expression from Isa 28:16 when he assures his addressees that a believer in Christ will not be let down (ὁ πιστεύων ἐπ' αὐτῷ οὐ καταισχυνθήσεται; Rom 9:33; 10:11). Similarly, in Rom 5:5, hope does not fail (ἡ δὲ ἐλπὶς οὐ καταισχύνει), and in 2 Cor 10:8 he claims that his boasting is valid, he will not lose face (οὐκ αἰσχυνθήσομαι). In 2 Cor 9:4 shame is for him, as well as for his addressees, to fail in the Jerusalem collection. Even his imprisonment will not lead to shame (ἐν οὐδενὶ αἰσχυνθήσομαι), meaning failure (Phil 1:20).

Outside of Paul, 1 Peter displays a similar pattern, quoting the same passage from Isaiah (ὁ πιστεύων ἐπ' αὐτῷ οὐ μὴ καταισχυνθῇ; 1 Pet 2:6). Believers who suffer, not for wrongs, but for their faith, should not be ashamed (μὴ αἰσχυνέσθω), that is, they should not regard this as a failure (1 Pet 4:16), and those who slander Christians will be "put to shame" (καταισχυνθῶσιν), that is, they will be proven wrong

---

[60] An association between secrecy and shame is also found in 2 Cor 4:2 (ἀπειπάμεθα τὰ κρυπτὰ τῆς αἰσχύνης).

[61] Lucian, *Dialogues of the Courtesans* 5.3.

[62] Cf. the similarly euphemistic use in Rom 1:27 and Rev 16:15 of ἀσχημοσύνη, which in the LXX is mainly found in Leviticus 18 and 20 and usually translates עֶרְוָה.

[63] Paul also reprimands the Corinthians (πρὸς ἐντροπὴν ὑμῖν λέγω), i.e., he shames them, for turning to outside judges (1 Cor 6:5) and for bad company leading to sin (1 Cor 15:33–34). However, in this context he does not employ αἰσχ-terminology,

(1 Pet 3:16).[64] Although the issue is Christian conduct (ἐν Χριστῷ ἀναστροφή), the shame mentioned does not concern or threat that conduct but the opponents, whose vilifications will fail.[65]

The examples I provide here are not comprehensive but representative enough. They demonstrate a primary focus for shame language in the New Testament: shame is a feeling of failure and defeat, the opposite of pride over success, and corresponds largely to the characteristics of SHAME II. We may register the cultural layers, but closely below them we detect an emotion inherited from our pre-human ancestors.

The other important focus for shame language in the New Testament is status and hierarchy. The unfaithful steward (οἰκονόμος) in Luke 16 is ashamed of the prospect of begging (ἐπαιτεῖν αἰσχύνομαι; 16:3); this would be below his status or dignity. Questions of status and hierarchy are also intrinsic to any discussions of gender roles, such as those already mentioned from 1 Timothy and 1 Corinthians. The context for Paul's discussion of hair length and head coverings in 1 Cor 11 has all to do with navigating earthly and heavenly hierarchies. A fixed hierarchy of "heads" is assumed, God – Christ – man – woman (παντὸς ἀνδρὸς ἡ κεφαλὴ ὁ Χριστός ἐστιν, κεφαλὴ δὲ γυναικὸς ὁ ἀνήρ, κεφαλὴ δὲ τοῦ Χριστοῦ ὁ θεός; 1 Cor 11:3), and the ways in which men and women cover their heads during prayer and prophecy are entirely related to this hierarchy (vv. 5–8).

Other hierarchies are overturned or inverted. Experiences that would normally be interpreted as failure, loss of control, and deprivation of status, are reinterpreted as signs of loyalty and success from a divine perspective of reversal. Paul claims that God elected the foolish and weak of the world in order to shame (καταισχύνη) the strong and wise, i.e., God reverses their status (1 Cor 1:27). Paul also warns believers against despising and "shaming" those of lower status, the have-nots (καταισχύνετε τοὺς μὴ ἔχοντας; 1 Cor 11:22). Numerous texts argue against feeling shame for involvement with issues and people below one's own status level. Paul is not ashamed of the gospel (οὐ γὰρ ἐπαισχύνομαι τὸ εὐαγγέλιον; Rom 1:16). According to Hebrews, God is not ashamed to be called the God of the faithful (διὸ οὐκ ἐπαισχύνεται αὐτοὺς ὁ θεὸς θεὸς ἐπικαλεῖσθαι αὐτῶν; Heb 11:16), Jesus is not ashamed

---

[64] συνείδησιν ἔχοντες ἀγαθήν, ἵνα ἐν ᾧ καταλαλεῖσθε καταισχυνθῶσιν οἱ ἐπηρεάζοντες ὑμῶν τὴν ἀγαθὴν ἐν Χριστῷ ἀναστροφήν.

[65] Several scholars have discussed the way in which 1 Peter turns shame into honour. See for example John H. Elliott, "Disgraced yet Graced: The Gospel according to 1 Peter in the Key of Honor and Shame," *Biblical Theological Bulletin* 25 (1995): 166–178; David A. DeSilva, "Turning Shame into Honor: The Pastoral Strategy of 1 Peter, in *The Shame Factor: How Shame Shapes Society* (ed. Robert Jewett; Eugene, OR: Cascade, 2011), 159–186.

of calling believers brothers (οὐκ ἐπαισχύνεται ἀδελφοὺς αὐτοὺς καλεῖν; Heb 2:11), and he was not even ashamed of the cross (ὑπέμεινεν σταυρὸν αἰσχύνης καταφρονήσας; Heb 12:2).[66]

Second Timothy talks repeatedly of the shame of imprisonment: the letter's "Paul" is not ashamed of his sufferings (δι' ἣν αἰτίαν καὶ ταῦτα πάσχω· ἀλλ' οὐκ ἐπαισχύνομαι; 2 Tim 1:12), Onesiphorus was not ashamed of "Paul's" imprisonment (τὴν ἅλυσίν μου οὐκ ἐπαισχύνθη; 2 Tim 1:16), and the author asks Timothy to be ashamed neither of the witness/suffering of the Lord, nor of him as a prisoner (μὴ οὖν ἐπαισχυνθῇς τὸ μαρτύριον τοῦ κυρίου ἡμῶν μηδὲ ἐμὲ τὸν δέσμιον αὐτοῦ; 2 Tim 1:8).

Even the synoptic Son of Man saying about reciprocal shame (Mark 8:38) fits into this pattern.

> ὃς γὰρ ἐὰν ἐπαισχυνθῇ με καὶ τοὺς ἐμοὺς λόγους ἐν τῇ γενεᾷ ταύτῃ τῇ μοιχαλίδι καὶ ἁμαρτωλῷ, καὶ ὁ υἱὸς τοῦ ἀνθρώπου ἐπαισχυνθήσεται αὐτόν, ὅταν ἔλθῃ ἐν τῇ δόξῃ τοῦ πατρὸς αὐτοῦ μετὰ τῶν ἀγγέλων τῶν ἁγίων.

> The person who is ashamed of me and my words in this adulterous and sinful generation, of him will the son of man be ashamed, when he comes in the glory of his father with the holy angels.

Without entering the discussion of how to relate "me" with the son of man,[67] we notice the plain message: recipients are encouraged not to feel shame for the lowly conditions of the earthly Jesus, but rather (as is clear from the preceding verses, Mark 8:34–37) to identify with them, because in the end the tables will be turned, and conditions reversed. Loyalty will, in other words, be rewarded.

In 1 John 2:28 we find a similar passage and some degree of influence either from Mark or from some related Jesus tradition is likely.[68] The recipients are encouraged to remain loyal in order to have confidence and not be shamed by him (referent unclear) at his appearance (μένετε ἐν αὐτῷ, ἵνα ἐὰν φανερωθῇ σχῶμεν παρρησίαν καὶ μὴ αἰσχυνθῶμεν ἀπ' αὐτοῦ ἐν τῇ παρουσίᾳ αὐτοῦ). It is a debated issue

---

[66] For a thorough socio-cultural analysis of shame language in the Epistle to the Hebrews, with an emphasis on reversal of values and a "corrective emphasis" on patronage, see David De Silva, *Despising Shame: Honor Discourse and Community Maintenance in the Epistle to the Hebrews*, rev. ed. (SBL Studies in Biblical Literature 21; Atlanta, GA: Society of Biblical Literature, 2008).

[67] Cf. Thomas Kazen, "Son of Man and Early Christian Identity Formation," in *Identity Formation in the New Testament* (ed. Bengt Holmberg and Mikael Winninge; WUNT 1:227; Tübingen: Mohr Siebeck, 2008), 97–122.

[68] Judith M. Lieu, *I, II, & III John: A Commentary* (NTL; Louisville, KY: Westminster John Knox, 2008), 115.

whether this verse closes the previous or introduces the subsequent section.[69] In the latter case, the references to righteousness in v. 29 may suggest a moral interpretation, so that the prospective shaming is associated with immoral behaviour, but there are strong reasons for v. 28 somehow pulling together the preceding christological section.[70] In that case, the text rather talks about loyalty to God/Christ ("remain in him") in contrast to those who listen to the antichrist. However, we must take a further aspect into account: the implications of the assurance or boldness (παρρησία) that is the opposite of being shamed. Although the term παρρησία often refers to frank (and critical) speech, and sometimes to rhetorical speech, or moral exhortation, this "freedom of speech" is rooted in the democratic right of citizens in classical Athens to express their views in the assembly. For many philosophers, such freedom was an inner virtue or capacity regardless of civic rights.[71] From this perspective, the contrast between παρρησία and shaming in 1 John 2:28 indicates two opposites with regard to status before the divine judge: subordinance shame versus integrity and positive self-evaluation, based on acceptance, even if not on equality. It could thus be argued that this passage reflects multi-faceted aspects of shame, but particularly attests to the predominance and paradigmatic nature of subordinance shame.

In sum, shame language in the New Testament is much less about social and moral norm infringement than many would expect. Expressions move along most of the shame continuum, but with dominance for frameworks represented especially by SHAME II and to some extent by EMBARRASSMENT II/SHAME I, in which issues of preventing or overcoming failure and defending or winning status are of crucial importance. Also in the New Testament, subordinance shame plays a major role.

Conclusions

Shame is a self-conscious emotion which contributes to the cooperation and survival of humanity, characterised as a highly advanced social species. Close to the

---

[69] For a review of various options and attempts, concluding there is no consensus at all, see Matthew D. Jensen, "The Structure and Argument of 1 John: A Survey of Proposals," *Currents in Biblical Research* 12 (2014): 194–215.

[70] Lieu, *I, II, & III John*, 114.

[71] Cf. essays in *Philodemus and the New Testament World* (ed. John T. Fizgerald, Dirk Obbink, and Glenn Stanfield Holland; SupNovT 111; Leiden: Brill, 2004); and essays in *Friendship, Flattery, and Frankness of Speech: Studies on Friendship in the New Testament World* (ed. John T. Fitzgerald; Leiden: Brill, 1996).

biological roots we find a subordinance shame which navigates social hierarchies and mitigates failures. The texts and contexts we have visited indicate and support an understanding of this type of "primordial" shame cutting across layers of cultural development and construction, making itself visible along much of the continuum of shame-related emotions. The majority of cases seem to reflect shame of the EMBARRASSMENT II/SHAME I and the SHAME II types. More often than not, shame means failure. Most conspicuously, shame is only occasionally associated with moral norm infringements, and then almost exclusively with trespasses of a sexual character and with transgressions of gender norms, which often also have hierarchical aspects and are status related.[72]

The texts and contexts we have discussed also suggest that social fear may play a more global role than we might think, as it has proved to be one of the underlying basic emotions associated with shame. Shame appears, in fact, as more visceral and closer to the basic emotions than we might have thought.

The cultural forms of shame, evidenced in the texts we have studied, accommodate to the highly hierarchical structures that dominated through the periods to which these texts belong. Some of these structures trace their roots far back into our primate past. Shame evolved for survival, but its social role is double-edged, or ambiguous. On the one hand, our capacity to feel shame facilitates cooperation and makes reciprocity and mutuality possible. This creates a problem for strongly individualistic cultures that often suppress shame. On the other hand, shame is easily and typically subsumed under hierarchical structures; shame is, in a sense, made for subordination and much of the history of humankind is ugly (αἰσχρός). Whether in the long run shame will assist human fellowship or ruin society is perhaps a political question, which does not belong here. But as long as an elbow in the food evokes more shame among the elite than rape and racism, there is still room for human culture to negotiate the biological substratum on which it grows.

Acknowledgement: The research for this article was funded by the Swedish Research Council, grant nr. 2016-02319.

---

[72] Cf. Thomas Kazen, *Smuts, skam, status: Perspektiv på samkönad sexualitet i Bibeln och antiken* (Göteborg: Makadam, 2018).

Law and Emotion in Moral Repair

Circumscribing Infringement

Introduction

The present article deals with the reciprocal relationship between law and emotion but is also framed by an ongoing project in which I am involved, dealing with Dynamics of Moral Repair in Antiquity.[1] With moral repair[2] we mean all sorts of reparations of interpersonal infringements, ranging from revenge and compensation to reconciliation and forgiveness. Such infringements involve compromised integrity and the transgression of boundaries which are seen as part of a divinely constituted moral order. They can take a number of forms: sexual infringements, property infringements, personal violence, violations of status and honour, and various other types of transgression against the social and hierarchical order, which in the ancient world was almost always understood to be divinely sanctioned.

The role of emotions for human interaction and morality has been emphasised in neuroscience (Antonio Damasio), primatology (Frans de Waal), and social psychology (Jonathan Haidt).[3] Haidt is known for his social intuitionist model, fol-

---

[1] The project "Moral Repair in Antiquity" (2017–2021) was funded by the Swedish Research Council and run by Rikard Roitto and Thomas Kazen.

[2] The concept of "moral repair" is borrowed from Margaret Urban Walker. Walker defines it as "the task of restoring or stabilizing – and in some cases creating – the basic elements that sustain human beings in a recognizably moral relationship" in *Moral Repair: Reconstructing Moral Relations after Wrongdoing* (Cambridge: Cambridge University Press, 2006), 23, or simpler, as in her subtitle ("reconstructing moral relations after wrongdoing"). Here it is used in a broad sense, as an umbrella term, for very diverse ways to handle moral infringements.

[3] Antonio R. Damasio, *Descartes' Error: Emotion, Reason and the Human Brain* (New York: Grosset/Putnam, 1994), which has become a classic; cf. idem, *The Feeling of What Happens: Body and Emotion in the Making of Consciousness* (New York: Harcourt Brace, 1999), and idem, *Looking for Spinoza: Joy, Sorrow, and the Human Brain* (Orlando, FL: Harcourt, 2003); and now, idem, *The Strange Order of Things: Life, Feeling, and the Making of Cultures* (New York:

lowed by the moral foundations theory, which indicate that a number of emotions are involved in moral appraisal, moral infringement, and moral repair. In this paper, I focus on sexual infringements and property infringements, and I emphasise the crucial role of hierarchy, which means that many infringements are ultimately also status infringements.

The model used for discussing moral infringements and their repair is evolutionary. Human behaviours and human emotions are deeply rooted in a prehistoric past, shared with other social species, primates in particular. They can be profitably understood and explained – at least in part – in terms of survival mechanisms or as strategies for individual or group success and survival (fitness). Needless to say, cultural constructs and constraints are decisive for shaping emotions and behaviours in historic contexts, to which law also belongs. An evolutionary perspective is also helpful for discussing infringements and their repair contextually, without anachronistically imposing modern values or moralising over ancient behaviour.[4]

Infringements and their repair can be conceptualised by various metaphorical frames and are appraised by a number of different emotions. I trace the influence of some of these emotions in the shaping of biblical law texts and the interaction between various emotions in legal reasoning and moral exhortation. I also discuss the process through which law regulates moral emotions and balances them, effectively curbing excess and avoiding disproportionate revenge. Finally, I point to the rhetorical function of law to bend and direct emotions in the service of moral values and social cohesion.

Pantheon Books, 2018). Frans B. M. de Waal, *Good Natured: The Origins of Right and Wrong in Humans and Other Animals* (Cambridge, MA: Harvard University Press, 1996; idem, *Chimpanzee Politics: Power and Sex among Apes*, rev. ed. (Baltimore, MD: Johns Hopkins Press, 1998 [1982]), idem, *The Age of Empathy: Nature's Lesson for a Kinder Society* (New York: Harmony Books, 2009). Jonathan Haidt, "The Emotional Dog and Its Rational Tail: A Social Intuitionist Approach to Moral Judgment," *Psychological Review* 108 (2001): 814–34; idem, "The Moral Emotions," in *Handbook of Affective Sciences* (ed. Richard J. Davidson, Klaus R. Scherer, and H. Hill Goldsmith; Oxford: Oxford University Press, 2003), 852–870; idem, *The Happiness Hypothesis: Putting Ancient Wisdom and Philosophy to the Test of Modern Science* (New York: Basic Books, 2006); idem, *The Righteous Mind: Why Good People are Divided by Politics and Religion* (New York: Pantheon Books, 2012).

[4] Some of the texts discussed in this essay raise legitimate questions – to the point of indignation – from other perspectives than biological adaptation and social dysfunction and I do acknowledge the importance of discussing them for example within discourses of justice, equality, and human rights. Here, however, I try to remain dispassionate and restrain my own values until the very end.

Moral Infringement and Emotions

Morality is a tricky concept. Anthropological and cross-cultural research have shown its contextual nature: it is a cultural construct and the distinction between morality and convention varies between times and cultures. Even when morality is understood as referring to issues crucial for the welfare of others and/or of society at large, behaviours that some cultures regard as amoral conventions are seen by others as crucial for the stability and survival of societies and individuals.[5] On the other hand, one can argue for certain universals, forming the basis for cultural constructions of morality, as in Jonathan Haidt's "moral foundations theory," which outlines six evolved cognitive modules that are correlated to various emotions.[6]

Haidt's theory has been problematised and criticised, not without reason,[7] but the moral foundations construct reminds us that morality is a complex concept which cannot simply be reduced to intuitive interpersonal regulations, based on human capacity for emotional empathy. Many other emotions are also involved in moral appraisal: anger, awe, disgust, fear, jealousy, pleasure, pride, and shame. An

---

[5] Richard A. Shweder, Manamohan Mahapatra, and Joan G. Miller, "Culture and Moral Development," in *The Emergence of Morality in Young Children* (ed. Jerome Kagan and Sharon Lamb; Chicago, IL: University of Chicago Press, 1987), 1–83; Noga Sverdlik, Sonia Roccas, and Lilach Sagiv, "Morality across Cultures: A Values Perspective," in *The Social Psychology of Morality: Exploring the Causes of Good and Evil* (ed. Mario Mikulincer and Philip R. Shaver; Washington, DC: American Psychological Association, 2012), 219–235; Joan G. Miller and Chloe G. Bland, "A Cultural Psychology Perspective on Moral Development," in *Handbook of Moral Development*, 2nd ed. (ed. Melanie Killen and Judith G. Smetana; New York: Psychology Press, 2014), 299–314.

[6] Haidt, *The Righteous Mind.* The modules are care/harm, fairness/cheating, loyalty/betrayal, authority/subversion, sanctity/degradation, and finally, liberty/oppression. The last module or moral foundation was added after the others, seemingly to keep Republican behaviour within a moral framework, and Haidt's scheme has been criticised by other theorists, among other things for not being that global, but rather American. Cf. Joshua Greene, *Moral Tribes: Emotion, Reason, and the Gap between Us and Them* (New York: Penguin Press, 2013) 334–346.

[7] Christopher Suhler and Patricia Churchland, "Can Innate, Modular 'Foundations' Explain Morality? Challenges for Haidt's Moral Foundations Theory," *Journal of Cognitive Neuroscience* 23 (2011): 2103–2116; Kathryn Iurino and Gerard Saucier, "Testing Measurement Invariance of the Moral Foundations Questionnaire Across 27 Countries," *Assessment (ASM)* 25/8 (2018): 1–8; Oliver Scott Curry, Matthew Jones Chester, and Caspar J. Van Lissa, "Mapping Morality with a Compass: Testing the Theory of 'Morality-as-Cooperation' with a New Questionnaire," *Journal of Research in Personality* 78 (2019): 106–124; Oliver Scott Curry, Daniel Austin Mullins, and Harvey Whitehouse, "Is It Good to Cooperate? Testing the Theory of Morality-as-Cooperation in 60 Societies," *Current Anthropology* 60 (2019): 47–69.

individual sense of fairness as well as a collective need for group belonging and group identity are equally important and emotionally grounded factors, influencing the behaviour and values of human beings. This means that we tend to experience as moral infringements not only transgressions directly affecting individual welfare, but also breaches against status and social order, as well as lack of compliance towards authorities and offence against divine powers.

In the ancient world, as in many places still today, the commonly accepted moral order more or less equalled the divine order, all set within a thoroughly hierarchical framework. Transgressions in the areas of sexuality, individual integrity, property, and justice were not different in principle from disloyalty and lack of subordination under authorities and hierarchical structures, whether human or divine.[8] As a result, not every killing, maltreatment, theft, or rape was considered sinful to the same degree, especially not when victims were seen as illegitimate, subordinate or outgroup. Instead, interpersonal infringements were at times considered sinful precisely when they transgressed divine or human authority, or when they upset hierarchical order. Hence, reactions against infringements must be understood as a blend of innate, biologically based, and contextual, culturally shaped emotions. Laws and regulations against infringements are likely to reflect such emotional involvement and conversely to promote their adherence by rhetorically triggering emotional engagement.

Evolutionary Perspectives on Emotions

The human species is a highly social one, dependent on advanced social interaction for survival and development. This creates numerous conflicts and instances of interpersonal infringement, in need of social and moral repair. Emotions play a key role in this, as they have evolved for adaptive functions through extremely long processes, to promote behaviours that lead to genetic success and survival.

We might perhaps expect the evolutionary process to have brought forward a well-adapted human race, but cultural evolution has outrun biological evolution from the neolithic period and onwards.[9] Behaviours that used to be advantageous

---

[8] Thomas Kazen, *Emotions in Biblical Law: A Cognitive Approach* (HBM 36; Sheffield: Sheffield Phoenix, 2011), chapter 3.

[9] I.e., the last 12 000 years, today also called the anthropocene. Cf. Kevin N. Laland, *Darwin's Unfinished Symphony: How Culture Made the Human Mind* (Princeton, NJ: Princeton University Press, 2017), 264–263. The fact that cultural evolution has proceeded at a much faster pace than biological evolution is usually taken for granted, but can also be argued from evidence, for

have become dysfunctional, even threatening our existence. Our instincts no longer protect us the way they supposedly did for our primate or even hunter-gatherer ancestors. Emotional reactions continue to make themselves known long after they ceased being functional. Many survival strategies have passed their best-before-date, since contexts have changed radically, as the small kin group has been exchanged for a global mega-city.[10] In fact, many prehistoric survival strategies were getting increasingly dysfunctional already when sedentary agricultural life was emerging and gaining ground.

Within the historic era of humanity, law emerges as a cultural construct, attempting to regulate interaction, infringement, and repair, so as to ensure continued cooperation, necessary for social survival. Every law does this within a particular context, which usually includes a hierarchic social structure. The basis for such legal regulation, however, is our emotional capacity. And since emotions have evolved to enhance the fitness of our species, they play on both sides as they are involved in both infringement and repair.[11]

Conceptual Metaphors for Moral Infringement and Repair

Moral infringements and moral repair can be conceptualised metaphorically in a number of ways, depending on our social and bodily experiences, and interacting with our emotions.[12] In various contexts, morality has been conceptualised by

---

example from an archaeological perspective. See Charles Perreault, "The Pace of Cultural Evolution," *Plos One* 7.9 (2012): 1–8.

[10] Evolutionary psychologists, human behavioural ecologists, and cultural evolutionists differ about the extent to which human beings display "maladaptive mismatches between cognitive adaptations and the environment," but all "agree that maladaptive behavioural responses can result from cultural processes." Gillian R. Brown and Peter J. Richerson, "Applying Evolutionary Theory to Human Behaviour: Past Differences and Current Debates," *Journal of Bioeconomics* 16 (2014): 105–128, (quotes from 110–111).

[11] De Waal, *Good Natured*; idem, *Empathy*, Cf. discussions in Thomas Kazen, "Self-Preserving and Other-Oriented Concerns in the Jesus Tradition," in *Voces Clamantium in Deserto: Essays in Honor of Kari Syreeni* (ed. Sven-Olav Back and Matti Kankaanniemi; Åbo: Teologiska fakulteten vid Åbo universitet, 2012), 124–148; idem, "Emotional Ethics in Biblical Texts: Cultural Construction and Biological Bases of Morality," *Hebrew Bible and Ancient Israel* 6 (2017): 434–459 (also in this volume).

[12] For conceptual metaphor theory in general, see Lakoff and Johnson, 1980, 1999. For the role of human bodily experiences for conceptualising and the notion of embodied cognitions, see Shapiro, 2014.

metaphors such as PATH, BURDEN, TRANSACTION, PURITY, BEAUTY, PROPOR-
TION, or POWER.[13]

Specifically, the first four, PATH, BURDEN, TRANSACTION, and PURITY, are
common conceptual metaphors in the Hebrew Bible for the human-divine relationship. Infringements against the divine order are like deviating from the right
path, like a burden, a debt, or like an impure state, while their repair is like return-
ing to the right road, alleviating the burden, settling the account, or purifying.
These conceptual domains are much less common as metaphors for interpersonal
infringements and repair.[14]

BEAUTY and PROPORTION are common conceptual domains in Greek philosophy, in which aesthetic aspects of morality stand in focus.[15] These metaphors are
more intent on character formation than on interpersonal moral repair. Something similar applies to POWER, or FORCE, which is a common conceptual metaphor for example in Stoic moral discourse. Here the focus lies on rationality and
(individual) control of the emotions,[16] again aiming at character formation, more
than interpersonal moral repair.[17]

When interpersonal relationships and integrity are in focus, however, the metaphors of MEASURE and SIZE stand out, especially in agonistic cultures, where
honour and status are important values within a hierarchical framework.[18]

---

[13] These are some of the conceptual metaphors for morality which we outline in our project;
Rikard Roitto and Thomas Kazen, *Interpersonal Infringement and Moral Repair: Revenge,
Compensation and Forgiveness in the Ancient World* (WUNT; Tübingen: Mohr Siebeck, forth-
coming 2023).

[14] Cf. Gary A. Anderson, *Sin: A History* (New Haven, CT: Yale University Press, 2009);
Joseph Lam, *Patterns of Sin in the Hebrew Bible: Metaphor, Culture, and the Making of a Religious Concept* (New York: Oxford University Press, 2016).

[15] Cf. David Konstan, *Beauty: The Fortunes of an Ancient Greek Idea* (New York: Oxford
University Press), 2014.

[16] Cf. John Sellars, *Stoicism* (Durham: Acumen, 2006), 110–120.

[17] For further discussion, see Roitto and Kazen, *Interpersonal Infringement and Moral Repair*, forthcoming.

[18] For overviews of honour as an important value in the ancient world, see for example Hal-
vor Moxnes, "Honor and Shame," *Biblical Theology Bulletin* 23 (1993): 167–176; David A. De-
Silva, *Honor, Patronage, Kinship & Purity: Unlocking New Testament Culture* (Downers Grove,
IL: InterVarsity Press, 2000), 23–42; Johanna Stiebert, *The Construction of Shame in the Hebrew
Bible: The Prophetic Contribution* (JSOTSup 346; Sheffield: Sheffield Academic Press, 2002), 25–
86; Richard L. Rohrbaugh, "Honor: Core Value in the Biblical World," in *Understanding the
Social World of the New Testament* (ed. Dietmar Neufeld and Richard E. DeMaris; London:
Routledge, 2010), 109–125.

MEASURE underlies many discourses about justice, distribution, compensation, and revenge. A basic sense of justice is found with many social species.[19] Chimps have temper tantrums when insulted or hindered by others, often resulting in revenge or negotiations.[20] Capuchins and chimps react against injustices, like when one in a pair receives a better reward than the other.[21] Dogs display similar behaviours.[22] Humans do too. We are most disturbed by *relative* deprivation, access to less resources than others in corresponding situations.[23] We also react to injustices against third persons.[24] A sense of justice seems to be universal.

MEASURE is a common conceptual metaphor in ancient texts for just distribution. It is useful for interhuman relationships and based on experiences of mutual respect and distribution of resources. MEASURE goes together with emotions like anger, envy, pain, and pleasure (cf. Aristotle, *Eth. nic.* 2.7.13). Moral infringements conceptualised by MEASURE may involve violence, damage, theft, fraud, and unfair distribution, infringements that can be repaired through compensation, revenge, or just be ignored, at least if the perpetrator is too powerful, or the opposite, not a threat at all. Most common is the talion principle, "an eye for an eye": pay the value of the damage, often together with a certain surplus compensation.[25]

SIZE can be understood as a concrete, spatial concept and an embodied social category. For many animals, it is important to estimate the size of the other to guess

---

[19] Sarah F. Brosnan, "Nonhuman Species' Reactions to Inequity and their Implications for Fairness," *Social Justice Research* 19.2 (2006): 153–185.

[20] De Waal, *Chimpanzee Politics*, 98–105; idem, *Peacemaking among Primates* (Cambridge, MA: Harvard University Press, 1989), 37–69; Brosnan, "Nonhuman Species," 155.

[21] Sarah F. Brosnan and Frans B. M. De Waal, "Monkeys Reject Unequal Pay," *Nature* 425 (2003): 297–299; eidem, "Fair Refusal by Capuchin Monkeys," *Nature* 428 (2004): 140; Brosnan, "Nonhuman Species," 170–179; Megan van Wolkenten, Sarah F. Brosnan, and Frans B. M. de Waal, "Inequity Responses of Monkeys Modified by Effort," *Proceedings of the National Academy of Sciences* 104 (2007): 18854–18859.

[22] Friederike Range, Lisa Horn, Zsófia Viranyi, and Ludwig Huber, "The Absence of Reward Induces Inequity Aversion in Dogs," *Proceedings of the National Academy of Sciences* 106 (2009): 340–345.

[23] Iain Walker and Heather J. Smith, *Relative Deprivation: Specification, Development, and Integration* (Cambridge: Cambridge University Press, 2002).

[24] Janne van Doorn, Marcel Zeelenberg, and Seger M. Breugelmans, "Anger and Prosocial Behavior," *Emotion Review* 6 (2014): 261–268; Janne van Doorn and Liewe Brouwers, "Third-Party Responses to Injustice: A Review on the Preference for Compensation," *Crime Psychology Review* 3 (2017): 59–77.

[25] Talion was often not applied literally; Hammurabi's law, for example, prescribes monetary compensation for injury of the lower classes, like the Covenant Code does for slaves. Hittite laws translate compensation for all injuries into fines in silver, cattle, or slaves. It may be that the translation of talion into a fixed pricelist goes together with centralisation and "government" control.

who will probably eat whom. For humans, size may indicate relative status, especially among men. Tall men earn more than short men on average and have advantages in mating and leadership positions.[26] In ancient iconography, gods were usually pictured as larger than humans, men larger than women, and free men as larger than slaves.[27]

We compare ourselves. We have experiences of body size relating to physical and social domination. The large and the strong receive more respect, climb higher in the hierarchy, and do not need to bother about the lower and the weak. This makes SIZE work as a metaphorical framework for status and position. Honour is high and large; shame is low and small. Feelings of pride or shame, superiority and confidence or inferiority, all relate to SIZE.[28] Moral infringements conceptualised

---

[26] Gert Stulp *et al.*, "A Curvilinear Effect of Height on Reproductive Success in Human Males," *Behavioral Ecology and Sociobiology* 66 (2012): 375–384; Nancy M. Blaker et al., "The Height Leadership Advantage in Men and Women: Testing Evolutionary Psychology Predictions about the Perceptions of Tall Leaders," *Group Processes & Intergroup Relations* 16 (2013): 17–27. Michael Baker and Kirsten Cornelson ("The Tall and the Short of the Returns to Height," *NBER Working Paper Series*; Working Paper 26325 (Cambridge, MA: National Bureau of Economic Research, 2019) modify the view that tall people have socioeconomic advantages; evidence rather suggest that short men have disadvantages, while exceeding mean height have little correlation with socioeconomic advantages for men and some correlation with advantages for women.

[27] Heinrich Schäfer, *Principles of Egyptian Art* (Oxford: Clarendon Press, 1974), 230–234, focusing on Egyptian art, comments on this: "Often we ourselves unconsciously approach tall people with a feeling of esteem and we use words of size both for physical size and inward, spiritual greatness. These are perhaps he traces, *transposed on to an aesthetic plane, of a residual feeling which goes back to a time when bodily strength still gave its possessors greater power than it does now*, that is to a time when the feeling of admiring awe before a healthy and massive physique was much stronger" (231; author's italics). Cf. Guitty Azarpay, "Designing the Body: Human Proportions in Achaemenid Art," *Iranica Antiqua* 29 (1994): 169–184, on Achaemenid art. Hierarchical proportions are generally assumed in literature on ancient iconography, see for example Stephanie Lynn Budin, *The Ancient Greeks: New Perspectives* (Santa Barbara, CA: ABC-CLIO, 2004), 226, on Minoan god iconography. Ann Macy Roth, "Little Women: Gender and Hierarchic Proportion in Old Kingdom Mastaba Chapels," in *The Old Kingdom Art and Archaeology: Proceedings of the Conference Held in Prague, May 31–June 4, 2004* (ed. Miroslav Bárta; Prague: Publishing House of the Academy of Sciences of the Czech Republic, 2006), 281–296, modifies the common view with regard to women.

[28] For "subordinance shame" expressed by a shrinking, or shrivelling posture, making oneself smaller, see Daniel M. T. Fessler, "From Appeasement to Conformity: Evolutionary and Cultural Perspectives on Shame, Competition, and Cooperation," in *The Self-Conscious Emotions: Theory and Research* (ed. Jessica L. Tracy, Richard W. Robins, and June Price Tangney; New York: Guilford Press, 2007), 174–193; Tara L. Gruenewald, Sally S. Dickerson, and Margaret E. Kemeny, "A Social Function for Self-Conscious Emotions: The Social Self Preservation Theory,

by this metaphor are about arrogance and abuse (*hubris*), shamefulness, and violations of integrity and status. Such infringements can be repaired by conciliatory gestures that restore the honour and status of the wronged party. This could be a matter of ransom, large or symbolic sums, which are not actually compensation according to the principle of talion, since honour and respect are immaterial values.[29] It is rather more important that perpetrators somehow bow their heads before the victim.

On the one hand, these metaphorical frameworks focus on different aspects of interpersonal infringements: MEASURE mainly relates to objects of conflict and their unjust distribution, while SIZE relates to the parties to a conflict and their asymmetrical relationship or disturbed equilibrium. On the other hand, the two frameworks are not clearcut, but often overlap and blend, since status and honour (SIZE) can also be conceptualised as transactional goods within the framework of MEASURE, while damage on, or the usurping of, another person's measurable resources (MEASURE) easily trigger feelings of outrage, of being demeaned and belittled (SIZE) – to seize the property of someone else is an act of domination. Hence these two frameworks cannot always be separated.

Laws for Moral Repair

Biblical law is closely related to ancient West Asian law – it is in fact an expression of it – but our extant examples of ancient West Asian law collections are much older than the Bible. It seems that these collections were not mainly for judicial purposes, but originate as literary exercises, royal apologia or otherwise ideological statements and as hypothetical exercises that could be used for reference and precedence. While not used for judging individual cases, they had a guiding function.[30]

---

in *The Self-Conscious Emotions: Theory and Research* (ed. Jessica L. Tracy, Richard W. Robins, and June Price Tangney; New York: Guilford Press, 2007), 68–87; cf. Thomas Kazen, "Viewing Oneself through Others' Eyes: Shame between Biology and Culture in Biblical Texts," *Svensk Exegetisk Årsbok* 84 (2019): 51–80, also in this volume.

[29] Cf. Jared Diamond, *The World Until Yesterday: What Can We Learn from Traditional Societies?* (London: Allen Lane, 2012), 89, about compensation in New Guinea: "the English word 'compensation,' … is misleading. The payment is actually a symbolic means to reestablish the previous relationship … what Billy's father really wanted was for Malo and his employers to acknowledge the great loss and grief that he had suffered." Cf. Kazen, *Emotions*, 149–162 on the practice of *kofer* in Israelite law.

[30] Both Hammurabi's law and the laws of Eshnunna are dated to the 18th century BCE, a millennium before the earliest reasonable dating of the Covenant Code. The Hittite laws are

The Hebrew *tôrâ* also means guidance, instruction, or teaching, rather than "law" in a judicial sense.[31] At the same time, along the process of canonization, the Torah gradually came to be viewed and applied as a legal document. This transition from formative ideal (or epistemic guidance) to normative legislation for a nation probably took place during the Hellenistic period, and the Greek understanding of *nomos* definitely had a more judicial meaning than the Hebrew *tôrâ*, as it can refer both to universal law and to a city's constitution.[32]

But the transformation from descriptive to prescriptive was a continuous process, during which the Torah gradually solidified. It could still to some extent be rewritten in environments like those reflected by the texts found in Qumran, but also interpreted in proto-halakic manner.[33] As it became more inflexible and prescriptive, it had to be negotiated by interpretative and often "legal formalist" (nominalist) exegesis, one law outweighing another, as with the rabbis.[34] The New

---

almost as old, although updated through several centuries, and the Middle Assyrian laws are dated to the 11th century BCE (Roth, 1997). One might question to what extent our term "law" is appropriate for the instructions of ancient West Asian "legal collections." While some rules come close to actual practice, others are hypothetical illustrations of typical cases, and some would represent a high degree of speculation aimed at exploring the borders or outer limits of certain judicial principles. Cf. Michael LeFebvre, *Collections, Codes, and Torah: The Re-characterization of Israel's Written Law* (LHB/OTS 451; New York: T. & T. Clark, 2006), 8–10; Jean-Louis Ska, *The Exegesis of the Pentateuch: Exegetical Studies and Basic Questions* (FAT 66; Tübingen: Mohr Siebeck, 2009), 196–220; Raymond Westbrook and Bruce Wells, *Everyday Law in Biblical Israel: An Introduction* (Louisville, KY: Westminster John Knox Press, 2009).

[31] Louis Isaac Rabinowitz, "Torah: The Term," *Encyclopedia Judaica*, 2nd ed. (ed. Fred Skolnik and Michael Berenbaum; Farmington Hills, MI: Macmillan Reference; Thomson Gale, 2007), 20: 139.

[32] LeFebvre, *Collections, Codes, and Torah*, for a summary, see 258–267; Jonathan Vroom, *The Authority of Law in the Hebrew Bible and Early Judaism: Tracing the Origins of Legal Obligation from Ezra to Qumran* (SupJSJ 187; Leiden: Brill, 2017), 66–73.

[33] Sidnie White Crawford, *Rewriting Scripture in Second Temple Times* (Studies in the Dead Sea Scrolls and Related Literature; Grand Rapids, MI: Eerdmans, 2008); *eadem*, "Scribal Traditions in the Pentateuch and the History of the Early Second Temple Period," in *Congress Volume Helsinki 2010* (*Vetus Testamentum* Supplement 148; ed. Martti Nissinen; Leiden: Brill, 2012), 167–184; Molly M. Zahn, *Rethinking Rewritten Scripture: Composition and Exegesis in the 4QReworked Pentateuch Manuscripts* (STDJ 95; Leiden: Brill, 2011).

[34] Aharon Shemesh, *Halakhah in the Making: The Development of Jewish Law from Qumran to the Rabbis* (The Taubman Lectures in Jewish Studies 6; Berkeley, CA: University of California Press, 2009); Thomas Kazen, *Scripture, Interpretation, or Authority? Motives and Arguments in Jesus' Halakic Conflicts* (WUNT 1:320; Tübingen: Mohr Siebeck, 2013). For an appeal to rather use the nomenclature "legal essentialist–legal formalist" than "realist–nominalist," see Aryeh Amihay, *Theory and Practice in Essene Law* (New York: Oxford University Press, 2017).

Testament is situated in the midst of this development.[35] Within the concept of law I would thus include not only Pentateuchal legal collections, but also rewritten and expanded legal texts, Qumran and rabbinic halakic elaborations, Greek Jewish informal interpretative accounts, and New Testament instruction and paraenesis.

Law as guidance or instruction, in all of these forms, often deals with interpersonal infringements and regulates emotional needs for moral repair of one or another sort. It both draws on various emotions to motivate its instructions and counteracts certain emotions to enable regulation and reparation, even though many texts may seem to lack emotions on the surface. Later elaborations often add little to the Pentateuchal laws with regard to emotions. Hence I will mainly discuss Pentateuchal texts, and only refer to their reception and elaboration in subsequent legal discussions when relevant for their emotional aspects.

Sexual Infringements

One of the issues that ancient laws address and try to regulate is human sexuality. From an evolutionary point of view, sex is a survival strategy for reproduction and an instinct older than *homo sapiens*. Sexual attraction is biologically based, although its cultural forms are contextual and socially constructed. Sexual pleasure is adaptive, as it facilitates procreation and increases fecundity.[36]

We can learn some things from our distant relatives. A new alpha male chimp has a tendency to kill infants of other males in order to make the females ready for his own mating with them. Female chimps, however, use a strategy of multiple matings to confuse paternity and thus limit infanticide. The less known bonobos are different in many regards. Sex is engaged in frequently, and females exercise a collective dominance over males. There is no infanticide within the group, but hostility to outgroup.[37]

---

[35] The Jesus tradition represents various stages on the way, but often reflecting an earlier understanding of law as instruction and guidance, in which there is no real conflict between the guidance and instruction of the Torah and its pragmatic application. Cf. Kazen, *Scripture* and idem, "Jesus and the Changing Role of the Torah," in preparation.

[36] In addition to this ultimate cause, sexual pleasure and attraction of course also has other functions. For a broad evolutionary account, see Michael R. Kauth, *True Nature: A Theory of Sexual Attraction* (New York: Kluwer Academic, 2000).

[37] During heat, female chimps usually mate 6–8 times a day, in full view of the group and with many males. In some species, multiple matings ensure male participation in infant care, but chimp males don't bother much. Towards the end of the females' swelling period, the most dominant male becomes overly possessive. In spite of this, females manage during heat to mate with

Homo sapiens have gone the opposite way. By bonding in pairs, like the Gibbons, they "ensure that they father their mate's offspring" and "repel infanticidal males – to protect their genetic investment."[38] Human offspring is vulnerable to the degree that male involvement in their care is demanded. Females are available not only during heat, which makes for closer bonds with males, but also for potential infidelity – the male had better take some responsibility. Compared to some other primates, humans are only mildly promiscuous. Human males need to cooperate for survival, so bonds between lower-ranking males and their mates are usually respected, too. This proto-nuclear family structure is based on paternity certainty.[39]

From an evolutionary perspective, certain infringements in the area of sex can be understood as originally functional survival strategies or adaptive behaviours that have become dysfunctional and out of context. What kind of sexual behaviours would evoke emotions and need regulation within a basically monogamous, but mildly promiscuous social species, where stable relationships are needed for the offspring's survival, where paternity certainty is ensured by pair bonding, where males need to cooperate for protein access, and where group cohesion protects against danger? Why would certain behaviours be regarded as social and moral infringements within their hierarchical framework? What behaviours would be reasonable and functional within a highly patriarchal culture?

---

multiple males, including those who mighty become the next alpha males. In this way, they confuse paternity and limit infanticide. Bonobos engage in sexual activities in all kinds of combinations and not only during heat, often to release tensions and reconcile. Females resume sexual activity very soon after childbirth, compared to chimps. There is no need for bonobo males to try to monopolise access to females. Paternity confusion becomes total and in-group infanticide is eliminated altogether. For thorough discussions with references to primary research, see Anne E. Pusey, "Of Genes and Apes: Chimpanzee Social Organization and Reproduction," in *Tree of Origin: What Primate Behavior Can Tell Us about Human Social Evolution* (ed. Frans B. M. de Waal; Cambridge, MA: Harvard University Press, 2001), 10–37; Frans B. M. de Waal, "Apes from Venus: Bonobos and Human Social Evolution," in *Tree of Origin* (ed. de Waal), 40–68; Richard B. Wrangham, "Out of the *Pan*, Into the Fire: How Our Ancestors' Evolution Depended on What They Ate," in *Tree of Origin* (ed. de Waal), 120–143.

[38] De Waal, "Apes from Venus," 63.

[39] The explanation is partly speculative, as the relative role of infanticide protection for pair bonding, compared to other possible advantages, such as mate guarding and parental care, is widely discussed. See for example Ryne A. Palombit, "Infanticide and the Evolution of Pair Bonds in Nonhuman Primates," *Evolutionary Anthropology* 7 (1999): 117–129.

Polygamy is presupposed in the Pentateuchal narratives.[40] From the perspective of SIZE as the metaphorical frame, polygamy is a privilege for alpha males, although it marks economic strength rather than body size. A main wife is complemented by concubines, paramours, or slaves, in a regulated form of (mild) promiscuity. Several women provide multiple opportunities for reproduction and indicate status and superiority for a man. But already when the patriarchal narratives were redacted, the system was being regarded somewhat dysfunctional, which for example the Jacob and Joseph cycles with all their intrigues exemplify.[41]

In the legal material polygamy is not the default setting but it does exist. Deut 21:15–17 (NRSV) reads:

> If a man has two wives, one of them loved and the other disliked, and if both the loved and the disliked have borne him sons, the firstborn being the son of the one who is disliked, then on the day when he wills his possessions to his sons, he is not permitted to treat the son of the loved as the firstborn in preference to the son of the disliked, who is the firstborn. He must acknowledge as firstborn the son of the one who is disliked, giving him a double portion of all that he has; since he is the first issue of his virility, the right of the firstborn is his.

The case is hypothetical (כִּי־תִהְיֶיןָ לְאִישׁ). Within the cultural context and its hierarchical system, fair distribution would mean twice as much for the first-born. Here various emotions clash. One wife is loved (הָאַחַת אֲהוּבָה), the other disliked (וְהָאַחַת שְׂנוּאָה). The double share of the first-born must nevertheless go to the son of the "hated" woman, if he is the oldest, since he is the "first/beginning of his strength/virility" (כִּי־הוּא רֵאשִׁית אֹנוֹ).[42] A sense of justice (MEASURE), within a particular hierarchical social structure where the first-born is seen as having "natural" privileges (SIZE), is assumed here, without being explicitly pronounced. It serves as an emotional check on a likewise emotional tendency to favour the son of the favourite wife. Law (מִשְׁפַּט הַבְּכֹרָה) thus circumscribes an infringement on the rights of the first-born, by implicitly enlisting culturally shaped emotions about just distribution over against other emotions working for partiality.

The composite role of emotions in regulating sexual infringements and repair can be illustrated by numerous legal texts from the Pentateuch. All have in

---

[40] The main patriarchs, Abraham and Jacob, have multiple wives and polygamy is assumed as a natural part of the narrative world.

[41] For example, in the conflict between Leah and Rachel, also involving their slave girls (Gen. 29–30) and the ensuing conflicts and intrigues between their sons (Gen 37; 42–45). Cf. also the conflict between Sarah and Hagar (Gen 16; 21).

[42] This is an adaptive argument of sorts, if the idea that the first offspring has a (natural/physical?) advantage is taken literally.

common that male sexuality has the prerogative but is regulated in line with the current cultural understanding and hierarchical social structure. For a man to penetrate another male of similar status (Lev 20:13),[43] or a woman under another man's control (Lev 20:10),[44] are acts of domination, which would be highly dysfunctional in a social context of interdependent and relatively equal men, and become an infringement, demeaning and shaming the other man (SIZE).[45] The two laws referred to here, satisfy a sense of justice (MEASURE) by condemning the people involved to death. They belong to the Holiness Code, parts of which are packed with disgust terms. The section is summarised by describing both God and the land as having emotions of disgust and vomiting out people behaving in such ways (קִיא, קוץ), and penetration of another male is explicitly called an "abomination."[46] Here again, the laws assume a hierarchical framework (SIZE) within which these infringements deserve the death penalty (MEASURE). An emotional common ground for authors and addressees is, however, implicit behind the legal reasoning and a necessary condition for the explicit rhetorical exploitation of disgust, in order to enlist an emotional response and obedient action from the addressees.

Emotions are not so often spelled out explicitly in the legal material. In the Covenant Code, they are at times slightly more visible on the textual surface than in the Holiness Code and in Deuteronomy. In the special case of the young man who finds (יִמְצָא) a girl who is *not* betrothed and seizes her (וּתְפָשָׂה), Deuteronomy dryly metes out a fine of 50 shekels to the father and orders the man to marry the girl and never divorce (Deut 22:28–29). In the Covenant Code, however, the non-engaged girl is seduced (יְפַתֶּה) rather than raped, which indicates there are more

---

[43] "If a man lies with a male as with a woman, both of them have committed an abomination; they shall be put to death; their blood is upon them" (Lev 20:13 NRSV).

[44] "If a man commits adultery with the wife of his neighbour, both the adulterer and the adulteress shall be put to death" (Lev 20:10 NRSV). Cf. the parallel "You shall not have sexual relations with your kinsman's wife, and defile yourself with her" (Lev 18:20 NRSV), and "If a man is caught lying with the wife of another man, both of them shall die, the man who lay with the woman as well as the woman. So you shall purge the evil from Israel" (Deut 22:22 NRSV). In their contexts, the two commands from the Holiness Code are associated with disgust, while the command from Deuteronomy has other overtones, see further below.

[45] Martti Nissinen, *Homoeroticism in the Biblical World: A Historical Perspective* (Minneapolis, MN: Fortress Press, 1998), esp. 37–56 on the Hebrew Bible; cf. Thomas Kazen, *Smuts, skam, status: Perspektiv på samkönad sexualitet i Bibeln och antiken* (Göteborg: Makadam, 2018), esp. 74–128 on status and subordination.

[46] תועבה, an H favourite term. Cf. Wilfried Paschen, *Rein und Unrein: Untersuchung zur biblischen Wortgeschichte* (SANT 24; Munich: Kösel-Verlag, 1971) 28–30; H. D. Preuß, "תּוֹעֵבָה tôʿēbâ; תעב tʿb," *TDOT*, vol. 15, rev. ed. (ed. Johannes Botterweck, Helmer Ringgren, and Heinz-Josef Fabry; Grand Rapids, MI: Eerdmans, 2006), 591–604.

complex emotions involved (Exod 22:15–16 [ET 16–17]). There is also the possibility that the father strongly refuses (מָאֵן יְמָאֵן) to give his daughter to this man is envisaged, and if so, he must pay bridewealth for a virgin as compensation anyway. We sense both lust and love, or at least a moment of infatuation, on the part of the young people,[47] and the father's refusal indicates a number of perhaps conflicting emotions, including a demand for compensation. The context is as patriarchal as always, but the frame perhaps more MEASURE than SIZE.

Both frames are involved when the Mishnah notes the difference between seduction and rape in these laws: the seducer is supposed to pay for the shame, the damage or discredit, and the fine (בֹּשֶׁת וּפְגָם וּקְנָס), while the rapist should also pay for the pain or grief (צַעַר) (m.Ket. 3:4). In the case of rape, there is more to be compensated for than imposed "subordinance shame" (SIZE),[48] namely the victim's pain and grief, implicitly motivated by empathy and a sense of justice (MEASURE).

Deuteronomy is often more restrained. In the same chapter 22, we find a commandment against sex with another man's wife, similar to the occurrences in the Holiness Code, but motivated by moral principle rather than disgust: "you shall purge the evil (הָרָע) from Israel" (Deut 22:22). The same motivation recurs for the young man who finds an *already* betrothed girl in the town and lies with her (Deut 22:23–24).[49] Both shall be stoned. In both cases, the infringement is clearly related to the hierarchical and patriarchal social construct: the woman is "the wife of

---

[47] פתה basically means "seduce," "entice." As Sandie Gravett points out, the verb פתה may take on connotations of violence (which I would suggest has to do with a general understanding in the ancient world of sexual intercourse within a framework of subduing and dominance). But even though "the possibility of sexual violence occurring in this context [Exod 22.15–16] cannot be dismissed," she nevertheless thinks that "a reading of rape lacks credibility." Sandie Gravett, "Reading 'Rape' in the Hebrew Bible: A Consideration of Language," *Journal for the Study of the Old Testament* 28.3 (2004): 279–299 (294–296; quote from 296).

[48] On shame in biblical texts and subordinance shame as paradigmatic, see Thomas Kazen, "Viewing Oneself through Others' Eyes: Shame between Biology and Culture in Biblical Texts," *Svensk Exegetisk Årsbok* 84 (2019): 51–80, also in this volume. Although we usually think of shame as a reaction to public failure – we realise that others are aware of our failure to comply with some moral or cultural standard – subordinance shame is more pristine and hierarchical, triggered basically by being viewed or brought to the attention of superiors, people of higher status. Cf. Daniel M. T. Fessler, "From Appeasement to Conformity: Evolutionary and Cultural Perspectives on Shame, Competition, and Cooperation," in *The Self-Conscious Emotions: Theory and Research* (ed. Jessica L. Tracy, Richard W. Robins, and June Price Tangney; New York: Guilford Press, 2007), 174–193.

[49] It is also the motivation for stoning the bride whose husband finds that she was not a virgin (Deut. 22:13–21).

another man" (בְעֻלַת־בַּעַל) (22:22). The innocent translation is "married to a hus-band," but the etymological and cultural meanings converge: she is subordinate, or lorded over by a lord. The betrothed girl is for all practical purposes viewed as a neighbour's wife (אֶת־אֵשֶׁת רֵעֵהוּ) (22:24), and the violation is described as a hum-bling (עַל־דְּבַר אֲשֶׁר־עִנָּה).[50] The SIZE frame dominates the discourse.[51] This, how-ever, implies underlying feelings of indignity and offence, which the law tries to amend by meting out the death penalty.

On one point does this law express emotional involvement: the betrothed girl's cry. If she is raped inside the town and did not cry for help, she is sentenced to death, but if in the countryside "the betrothed girl cried, but there was no helper for her" (Deut 22:27: צָעֲקָה הַנַּעֲרָ הַמְאֹרָשָׂה וְאֵין מוֹשִׁיעַ לָהּ). But in spite of what seems like an obvious trigger for empathy, the law is rather matter-of-fact: the cry is only a tool to decide guilt. The psychological fact that being attacked could make a person numb and silent is never considered.[52]

Within a tight-knit and vulnerable social group it would be quite dysfunc-tional to allow alpha males to seize other men's women at their wish. But one might find it as dysfunctional to diminish the size and strength of the social group by death penalty for such infringements, and in actual practice we may suspect that various types of compensations were agreed upon (less disproportional

---

[50] One could argue that the text views the infringement as more than an injury against male honour, since the rape is likened to an assault and murder (v. 26). But the abasement of the girl is clearly understood as an infringement on her father's honour, as the example in vv. 28–29 shows, where the father is the recipient of the fine. Cf. Gravett, "Reading 'Rape'," 285–286. Although the verb ענה does at times carry violent connotations, males often establish their honour (or per-sonhood) by violent means and sexual acts are often conceptualised and described with violent and possessive vocabulary in ancient texts. This is not to tone down the role of physical violence in such an act – which we appropriately call rape – but only to emphasise the humbling or sham-ing aspect. Cf. Johanna Stiebert, "Divinely Sanctioned Violence Against Women: Biblical Mar-riage and the Example of the *Sotah* of Numbers 5," *The Bible & Critical Theory* 15.2 (2019): 83–108 (87). On violence and personhood, see Tracy M. Lemos, *Violence and Personhood in Ancient Israel and Comparative Contexts* (Oxford: Oxford University Press, 2017).

[51] Deuteronomy presents an exception to the last case when the rape takes place outside of the town. In the town the girl should have cried for help, but outside the town she might have cried without anybody hearing her; hence she is not deemed guilty (Deut 22:25–27).

[52] Dissociation and freezing are somatic trauma responses when fight or flight seem impossi-ble; cf. Robert Scaer, *The Body Bears the Burden: Trauma, Dissociation, and Disease*, 3rd ed. (New York: Routledge, 2014), 7–20.

applications of the frame of MEASURE).[53] However, such compromises would be complicated by strong emotional demands for revenge, as Prov 6:32–35 (NRSV) explains:

> But he who commits adultery has no sense; he who does it destroys himself. He will get wounds and dishonour, and his disgrace will not be wiped away. For jealousy arouses a husband's fury, and he shows no restraint when he takes revenge. He will accept no compensation, and refuses a bribe (כֹּפֶר) no matter how great.[54]

Adultery is associated with feelings of honour and shame, within a hierarchical social context. The envy and fury which Proverbs takes for granted are made invisible in Deuteronomy's law. Are we supposed to sense it below the surface? Is it repressed as part of Deuteronomy's attempt to bring jurisdiction under central control and common practice?

This is not to say that Deuteronomy's sex laws are totally without emotions. In the same chapter 22, we find the case of the bridegroom who comes to "hate" (שְׂנֵאָה) his new wife after having tried her in bed and decides that she was no virgin (Deut 22:13–21). As distasteful to modern Western minds as the practice of providing material evidence for "virginity" is, the law could be understood to regulate and hinder injustice, based on strong emotions of aversion.[55] Similarly, but with many more emotions on the surface, Num 5:12–31 about the *sotah*, forced to drink curse water, could be seen as an attempt to circumscribe one infringement – wife murder, because of an imagined infringement due to pathological jealousy – by legal regulation. Such an interpretation may be too benevolent, however,[56] not

---

[53] Cf. the fact that Josephus, the Pharisees, and later the rabbis, seem to have assumed or demanded monetary settlement as an alternative to talion in many cases. For further discussion and references, see Kazen, *Emotions*, 142–149.

[54] The term כֹּפֶר in this context is often translated as "bribe," but this can be questioned, if כֹּפֶר is understood as a symbolic token of acknowledgement and submissiveness, rather than full restitution. See the discussion above.

[55] Cf. Mark E. Biddle, *Deuteronomy* (Smyth & Helwys Bible Commentary; Macon, GA: Smyth & Helwys, 2003), who notes the focus on paternity certainty and thinks "the double standard is appalling," although he suggests that the cases in Deut 22:13–30 (including this case of accusing the newly wed woman) "demonstrate an interest, not only in defending the reproductive 'rights' of men, but also in protecting women against men who would take advantage of the power inequality between the sexes." He quickly adds, however, that this is a very limited form of protection (337). Many commentators do not even mention such aspects.

[56] Cf. Cecilia Wassén, *Women in the Damascus Document* (Academia Biblica 21; Atlanta, GA: Society of Biblical Literature, 2005), 61–63, criticising Milgrom and others for a too "optimistic reading." See also Stiebert, "Divinely Sanctioned Violence," who discusses the *sotah* ritual in the context of gender-based violence, including intimate partner violence, today, and the exposure of women in law courts.

least in view of how rabbinic texts explain its application.[57] The law rather circum-scribes something that within its specific type of patriarchal context would be a dysfunctional behaviour, namely multiple mating, causing paternity uncer-tainty.[58] The passage bristles with emotions: envy, anger, disappointment, disgust (impurity language), and fear.

The text makes it clear that the punishment includes infertility, perhaps mis-carriage, while vindication means the woman will remain fertile (וְנִזְרְעָה זָרַע) (Num 5:28), perhaps "retain her seed" (וְנִזְרְעָה זָרַע) (Num 5:28). Although it does not explicitly say that the woman is already pregnant, a text from Qumran seems to interpret her so (4Q270 4, line 4).[59] This fits with what we have indicated above about the need for paternity certainty. The fear of foreign genes in the family group comes to the surface in a passage in Sirach about "a woman who leaves her husband and presents him with an heir by another man" (γυνὴ καταλιποῦσα τὸν

---

[57] Mishnah Sotah provides a disturbing description of the ritual, which one would hope is not historical, but nevertheless revealing for what a patriarchal society could imagine regarding the treatment of a suspected woman.

> If she said, "I am defiled to you", she gives him a receipt for her ketubah and goes out [with a get]. But if she says, "I am pure", they bring her up to the east gate, Nicanor's gate, where they give women suspected of adultery the water to drink, purify women after childbirth and purify lepers. A priest seizes her clothing, if they are torn, then they are torn, and if they become unstitched, then they are unstitched, until he uncovers her bosom, and he undoes [the braids of] her hair. Rabbi Judah says: if her bosom was beau-tiful he does not uncover it, and if her hair was beautiful he does not undo it. If she was clothed in white, he clothes her in black. If she wore gold jewelry or necklaces, ear-rings and finger-rings, they remove them from her in order to make her repulsive. After that [the priest] takes a rope made of twigs and binds it over her breasts. Whoever wishes to look upon her comes to look with the exception of her male and female slaves, since she has no shame in front of them. All of the women are permitted to look upon her, as it is said, "That all women may be taught not to do after your lewdness" (m. Sotah 1:5–6; transl. sefaria.org).

The tractate's first three chapters make it very clear that the purpose of the rite, as it was under-stood at the time of the *Tannaim*, was to shame the suspect and try to force her to confess.

[58] That the secret sowing of another man's seed is the issue at stake is indicated by the word-ing of the phrase וְשָׁכַב אִישׁ אֹתָהּ שִׁכְבַת־זָרַע (Num 5:13). The magical character of the ordeal is emphasized by Baruch A. Levine, *Numbers 1–20* (AB 4A; New York: Doubleday, 1993), 205–212.

[59] לֹא יִב]יֹאֹה כִי אם דמה יצוֹא [. The negation is conjectured. For a discussion, including a comparison with rabbinic interpretation, see Wassén, *Women*, 62–63, 65–67. Sexual infringe-ment is a common topic in Qumran texts, not least in the rule texts, but usually with a focus on the deviating practices of the community's opponents, on forbidden relationships, and on ritual purity issues. When the main biblical laws regarding sexual infringements are referred, the Scroll texts rarely go beyond the Pentateuchal texts.

ἄνδρα καὶ παριστῶσα κληρονόμον ἐξ ἀλλοτρίου; Sir 23:22).[60] The rabbis suggest that this is part of their interpretation of the *sotah* passage by stating that women who cannot conceive do not drink the water (m. Sotah 4:3).[61] However, neither wife murder, nor infanticide, would be adaptive behaviour in human social groups. In as far as the rite prevents this, it could be seen as regulating strong emotions related to the SIZE frame and negotiating them with others, related to MEASURE.

All of this is valid for the in-group, but not for outgroup. Further on in Numbers (31:17–18), we find the law prescribing both genocide and infanticide of Midianites, with the exception of untouched girls. The strategy is logical from a certain point of view: Virgins will be an asset to the group, without transmitting any outgroup lineage, while foreign males would compete for resources, including in-group women.[62] The law enlists the rage of Moses (וַיִּקְצֹף מֹשֶׁה) to reinforce the point, but no other emotions are indicated. Any traces of empathy would be counterproductive to the purpose of this command.

Property Infringements

Another adaptive strategy through the evolutionary process is to acquire resources necessary for survival. The most basic example is intake of food, but human beings also need shelter, warmth, tools, and various types of reserves to ensure future survival. Nature provides most of this for the hunter-gatherer, although resources may vary. In more advanced and complex societies there are further aspects.

Research on prehistoric societies is necessarily speculative and draws heavily on studies of still existing remains of hunter-gatherers.[63] They often have a flat structure, not much of hierarchy, and share resources without anyone trying to

---

[60] Her offence is threefold, according to Sir 23:23: she has disobeyed the law of the Highest, she has offended her husband, and she has "committed adultery by fornication" and "presented children by another man" (ἐν πορνείᾳ ἐμοιχεύθη καὶ ἐξ ἀλλοτρίου ἀνδρὸς τέκνα παρέστησεν).

[61] "A sterile woman and an old woman and a one who is not fit bear children do not drink" (אַיְלוֹנִית וּזְקֵנָה וְשֶׁאֵינָהּ רְאוּיָה לֵילֵד, לֹא שׁוֹתוֹת).

[62] Modern examples of genocide combined with rape and abduction of young women are easy to find, for example in the recent ravages of ISIS.

[63] On the development of "ethnoarchaeology," see Paul J. Lane, "Hunter-Gatherer-Fishers, Ethnoarchaeology, and Analogical Reasoning," in *The Oxford Handbook of the Archaeology and Anthropology of Hunter-Gatherers* (ed. Vicki Cummings, Peter Jordan, and Marek Zvelebil; Oxford: Oxford University Press, 2014), 104–150.

acquire more than is reasonable. If someone tries there are sanctions.[64] Paradoxically, such "egalitarian" groups can exercise domination and violence against competing groups, especially if resources are scarce. Then others' assets become potential resources for the survival of one's own group. In the struggle for survival, threat, coercion, and lethal violence, may be viewed as legitimate. In this area, too, interesting comparisons can be made with other primates.[65]

Property, in a modern sense, was hardly an issue during *homo's* prehistory, and is hardly relevant for hunter-gatherers. Property becomes a concept during the sedentary phase of human life, with division of labour and hierarchical structures.[66] Hierarchies rest on recognition of status, which can be built by resources such as property, power, and authority. "Modern" (in contrast to prehistoric) societies develop social strata or classes with elites, free men and women, and various subordinate categories, including slaves. Our basic sense of justice requires relative equity within the subgroup (among equals), while diverse conditions can be accepted between the groups. Too big differences, however, create tensions that may get out of hand.

In contrast to small and relatively egalitarian hunter-gatherer bands, more advanced societies tolerate a higher degree of individualism and inequality. Certain individuals are able to acquire large and disproportionate shares of available resources. Threat, coercion, and violence can still be used, but not in any manner. Superiors have rights and can take liberties that subordinates cannot. But ways to distribute and redistribute resources between various subgroups are mainly built into the systems. Occasionally conflicts flare up between subgroups and in con-

---

[64] James Woodburn, "Egalitarian Societies," *Man* 17 (1982): 431–451; idem, "Egalitarian Societies Revisited," in *Ritualisation, Sharing, Egalitarianism*; vol. 1 of *Property and Equality* (ed. Thomas Widlok and Wolde Gossa Tadesse; New York: Berghahn Books, 2005), 18–31. On food sharing among hunter-gatherers in comparison with non-human primates, cf. Mitsuo Ichikawa, "Food Sharing and Ownership among Central African Hunter-Gatherers: An Evolutionary Perspective," in *Ritualisation* (ed. Widlok and Tadesse), 151–164. See also other articles in *Ritualisation* (ed. Widlok and Tadesse).

[65] For an interesting overview and discussion of theories of "parochial altruism" (the relationship between intergroup conflict and intragroup altruism) in humans, including comparison with other primates, which also presents (complementing) alternatives to the standard view, see Hannes Rusch, "The Evolutionary Interplay of Intergroup Conflict and Altruism in Humans: A Review of Parochial Altruism Theory and Prospects for Its Extension," *Proceedings of the Royal Society B* 281 (2014): 20141539, 1–9.

[66] Samuel Bowles and Jung-Kyoo Choi, "Coevolution of Farming and Private Property During the Early Holocene," *Proceedings of the National Academy of Sciences* 110 (2013): 8830–8835.

flicts between societies, nations, and civilisations, there is still competition – in war everything is permitted.

Hence the seizure of resources through violence and abuse triggers strong emotions and mechanisms of protection and revenge. To retaliate means to protect one's body, integrity, status, and life. Revenge is universal, not limited to primates, but even found among fish, like guppies.[67] Deterrence warns potential aggressors. But the larger and more complex a society becomes, the stricter regulations we need for these things. To balance between cooperation and competition is tricky for a social species. The larger the contexts get, the more dysfunctional it becomes to acquire resources through dominance and violence, especially when they are no longer needed for survival, but rather for increasing and maintaining status.

Through history, groups as well as individuals have tried to outcompete each other, in a fight for scarce resources, such as arable land, water, and animals, or for resources imagined to be scarce.[68] To seize the resources of an outgroup could give an important contribution to subsistence for those who were superior in strength or could keep away afterwards, but often proved dangerous. For individuals it could be disastrous. The Pentateuchal laws regulate such property infringements as we would call theft. We find an example towards the end of the Decalogue (Exod 20:15–17 NRSV):[69]

> You shall not steal. You shall not bear false witness against your neighbour. You shall not covet your neighbour's house; you shall not covet your neighbour's wife, or male or female slave, or ox, or donkey, or anything that belongs to your neighbour.

The reference to the neighbour's wife, and possibly to his slave, too, might have been included in our previous discussion about sexual infringements. Here we will consider the property aspect of the commandment.[70] Within the assumed patriarchal framework and in the social reality represented by the text, all of the "items" mentioned have in common that they are under the control of a free male householder.

---

[67] Michael McCullough, *Beyond Revenge: The Evolution of the Forgiveness Instinct* (San Francisco: Jossey-Bass, 2008), 74–87, with references to studies on various animals.

[68] Tracy M. Lemos, "Dispossessing Nations: Population Growth, Scarcity, and Genocide in Ancient Israel and Twentieth-Century Rwanda," in *Ritual Violence in the Hebrew Bible: New Perspectives* (ed. Saul M. Olyan; New York: Oxford University Press, 2015), 27–65.

[69] The Holiness Code has it similarly: "You shall not steal; you shall not deal falsely; and you shall not lie to one another. And you shall not swear falsely by my name, profaning the name of your God: I am the Lord. You shall not defraud your neighbour" (Lev 19:11–13 NRSV).

[70] However, without implying that women would have been regarded as property in the same way as slaves. See the discussion in Lemos, *Violence and Personhood*, 61–98.

An underlying emotion is indicated: the verb for "covet," חָמַד, means to "desire," "to take delight in," or "to appropriate." There is a positive and a negative notion. We might interpret it partly as lust in relation to the neighbour's woman, but mainly as envy, jealousy, and greed in relation to the total resources of the neighbour, who is another free male with similar position and status. One part of your survival instinct wants to seize your neighbour's resources, to enhance your own power and status. This, however, requires enough strength to begin with, which may perhaps be possible for a ruler. King David can have Uriah killed to take Batsheba, and king Ahab can have Naboth stoned to take his vineyard (2 Sam 11; 2 Kings 21). The SIZE frame is at work here, but a neighbour is as large as you are. Between peers or equals such infringements lead to social disruption and even when committed by superiors or rulers, they are emotionally unacceptable to our sense of justice (MEASURE). This is reflected in 1 Sam 12:3 (NRSV), where the prophet asks the people:

> Whose ox have I taken? Or whose donkey have I taken? Or whom have I defrauded? Whom have I oppressed? Or from whose hand have I taken a bribe to blind my eyes with it? Testify against me and I will restore it to you.

Theft in ancient law is usually regulated by compensation, including a certain surplus. Emotional aspects are, however, seldom indicated or implied. The Covenant Code (Exod 21–23) regulates among other things various types of property infringement: theft and burglary (21:37–22:3 [ET 22:1–4]), damage on crops (22:4–5 [ET 5–6]), theft and damages during safekeeping (22:6–7, 9–12 [ET 7–8, 10–13]), disputed ownership (22:8 [ET 9]), damages during borrowing and hiring (22:13–14 [ET 14–15]). The closest parallels to these laws are found in the 18th century BCE laws of Eshnunna and especially of Hammurabi. A common trait between some of these laws and some of the Pentateuchal laws is that compensation exceeds the value of the stolen animal or stolen goods. In the Covenant Code an ox is compensated with five oxen and a sheep with four sheep, if the animal has been sold or slaughtered. If found alive, double compensation suffices (Exod 21:37; 22:3 [ET 22:1, 4]). Other laws stipulate monetary fines, capital punishment, or compensation up to thirty times the stolen item, in certain cases.[71] Although the gravity of the punishment could be understood to signal the degree of emotional indignation at various infringements, this is never even hinted at on the textual surface. The allowance made for killing a thief at night, but not during daylight,[72] suggests fear

---

[71] LE 23, 49 (stolen slaves); LH 8, 12, gap w, 106–107, 112, 120, 124, 254, 265.

[72] Exod 22:1–2 (ET 2–3); cf. LE 12–13.

of life during night, when one cannot appraise the situation properly, but this is only to be assumed.

Fear must also be assumed as an underlying emotion in CD IX, 10b–12, which elaborates on Exod 22:6–8 (ET 7–9).[73] The statement that the master of the house shall be brought before (the) god(s) (וְנִקְרַב בַּעַל־הַבַּיִת אֶל־הָאֱלֹהִים) is interpreted in terms of an oath.[74] The *Damascus Document* (CD IX, 11–12) reads: "its owner shall cause to be pronounced an oath curse. And he who hears it, if he knows and does not tell, shall bear guilt."[75] The oath thus acts as a deterrent against withholding information. As in the case of the *sotah*, the curse is supposed to scare those involved to compliance.[76] Although private property was restricted in the *Yaḥad*, the *Community Rule* also deals with property infringements (1QS VI, 18–23): negligence with community property entails replacement or punishment (1QS VII, 6–8), while lying regarding possessions leads to both temporary exclusion and reduced food rations (1QS VI, 24–25). Threats of punishment always imply emotional involvement, but the form and phrasing is quite austere. Leviticus' instructions about the *asham* sacrifice in cases of theft and safekeeping (Lev 5:21–26 [ET 6:2–7]),[77] have sometimes been interpreted as the perpetrator experiencing or *feeling* guilt for his action, but the translation of וְאָשֵׁם is controversial: does the man realise his guilt, is he convicted, or does he actually *feel* guilt and repent?[78] I suspect the last alternative of being anachronistic,[79] and suggest that here, too, the

---

[73] For a convincing discussion of the intertextual relationship, see Shlomo Zuckier, "The Neglected Oaths Passage (CD IX:8–12): The Elusive, Allusive Meaning," in *Hā-'tsh Mōshe: Studies in Scriptural Interpretation in the Dead Sea Scrolls and Related Literature in Honor of Moshe J. Bernstein* (ed. Binyamin Y. Goldstein, Michael Segal, and George J. Brooke; STDJ 12; Leiden: Brill, 2018), 343–362.

[74] Zuckier ("The Neglected Oaths Passage," 350) points out the similar assumption made in rabbinic texts (*Mekhilta* to Exod. 22:7; b. B. Qam. 63b). Cf. 1 Kings 8:31–32.

[75] Transl. Baumgarten and Schwartz, in *Damascus Document, War Scroll, and Related Documents* (The Dead Sea Scrolls 2; ed. James H. Charlesworth; Tübingen: Mohr Siebeck, 1995).

[76] The role that religious beliefs in being monitored by (a) supernatural agent(s) play for compliance and cooperation is subject to much anthropological, biological, psychological, and neuroscientific research. Cf. Dominic Johnson, *God Is Watching You: How the Fear of God Makes Us Human* (New York: Oxford University Press, 2016).

[77] Here only 20% is added to the full compensation of the value of the damage.

[78] Jacob Milgrom, "The Priestly Doctrine of Repentance," *Revue Biblique* 82 (1975): 186–205; idem, *Cult and Conscience: The Asham and the Priestly Doctrine of Repentance* (SJLA 18; Leiden: Brill, 1976).

[79] David A. Lambert, *How Repentance Became Biblical: Judaism, Christianity, and the Interpretation of Scripture* (New York: Oxford University Press, 2016).

emotional aspect is only implicit, in that reparation satisfies a sense of fairness (MEASURE) and a submission to status loss (SIZE).

Emotions are much more visible on the surface in the apodictic laws in the Covenant Code (Exod 22:20–26 [21–27]), which in contrast to the the preceding casuistic *mishpatim* are less dependent on other ancient legal collections,[80] although they certainly have themes in common: the foreigner, the widow, and the orphan are well-known topics.[81] These categories must not be maltreated or humbled – when they cry God will certainly listen (Exod 22:21–22 [ET 22–23]). The language is forceful, with three infinite absolutes paired with finite verbs of the same roots, expressing certainty or intensity (אִם־עַנֵּה תְעַנֶּה אֹתוֹ כִּי אִם־צָעֹק יִצְעַק אֵלַי שָׁמֹעַ אֶשְׁמַע צַעֲקָתוֹ). God is understood to sympathise with the emotional plight of vulnerable categories of people: his anger will flame (חָרָה אַפִּי) and he will avenge them (22:23 [ET 24]). This includes infringements on their minimal property – here is the context for the ban against interest on loans (22:24 [ET 25]) – so that even if one takes a neighbour's cloak in pawn, one must return it before sunset (22:25 [ET 26]). The motivation is strongly emotional (22:26 [ET 27]):

כִּי הוּא (כְסוּתהֹ) [כְסוּתוֹ] לְבַדָּהּ הוּא שִׂמְלָתוֹ לְעֹרוֹ בַּמֶּה יִשְׁכָּב וְהָיָה כִּי־יִצְעַק אֵלַי וְשָׁמַעְתִּי כִּי־חַנּוּן אָנִי

for this is his covering garment, this is what he wraps his skin in, in what will he sleep? So when he cries out I will listen, for I am compassionate.

Empathy, then, as a divine emotion and as part of the MEASURE frame, cuts through concerns for justice more in line with the SIZE frame. Claims on a person's ultimate property, while formally just, are deemed ultimately unreasonable and a divine threat looms large over those who pursue them. The theme turns up again in Lev. 19:13, although here it is without emotional rhetorical overtones, and it is prominent in Sirach, who strengthens the association between exploiting vulnerable categories and property infringements (Sir 34:20–22 [ET 24–27]):

[20] θύων υἱὸν ἔναντι τοῦ πατρὸς αὐτοῦ ὁ προσάγων θυσίαν ἐκ χρημάτων πενήτων

[21] ἄρτος ἐπιδεομένων ζωὴ πτωχῶν ὁ ἀποστερῶν αὐτὴν ἄνθρωπος αἱμάτων

[22] φονεύων τὸν πλησίον ὁ ἀφαιρούμενος ἐμβίωσιν καὶ ἐκχέων αἷμα ὁ ἀποστερῶν μισθὸν μισθίου

---

[80] Summary in Kazen, *Emotions*, 56–61, 96–97.

[81] Cf. LH Epilogue xlvii 59–62, in which Hammurabi claims to have set up his laws to protect the weak, the widow and the homeless girl. David Wright finds the weak in LH comparable to the foreigner in the Covenant Code: both categories are socioeconomically disadvantaged and powerless. David P. Wright, *Inventing God's Law: How the Covenant Code of the Bible Used and Revised the Laws of Hammurabi* (Oxford: Oxford University Press, 2009), 57–58, 379 n.21).

[24] Like one who kills a son before his father's eyes is the person who offers a sacrifice from the property of the poor.

[25] The bread of the needy is the life of the poor; whoever deprives them of it is a murderer.

[26] To take away a neighbour's living is to commit murder; [27] to deprive an employee of wages is to shed blood. (NRSV)

Extortion, exploitation, and deprivation is here likened to bloodshed. In this way, the rhetoric appeals to disgust, anger, indignation, and a sense of justice, without mentioning a single emotion. A little further on in the text, Sirach mediates the divine perspective: God is not partial but listens to the orphan and the widow (35:13–14 [ET 16–17]). "Do not the tears of the widow run down her cheek as she cries out against the one who causes them to fall?" (οὐχὶ δάκρυα χήρας ἐπὶ σιαγόνα καταβαίνει καὶ ἡ καταβόησις ἐπὶ τῷ καταγαγόντι αὐτά; 35:15 [ET 18–19] NRSV). Here emotions are right on the surface.

Whether emotions had any place in legal discussions was a contested issue already in antiquity. A story from m. Ketub. 9:2 reads (transl. sefaria.org),

מִי שֶׁמֵּת וְהִנִּיחַ אִשָּׁה וּבַעַל חוֹב וְיוֹרְשִׁין, וְהָיָה לוֹ פִקָּדוֹן אוֹ מִלְוָה בְּיַד אֲחֵרִים, רַבִּי טַרְפוֹן אוֹמֵר, יִנָּתְנוּ לַכּוֹשֵׁל שֶׁבָּהֶן. רַבִּי עֲקִיבָא אוֹמֵר, אֵין מְרַחֲמִין בַּדִּין

> A man died and left a wife, a creditor, and heirs and he also had a deposit or a loan in the possession of others: Rabbi Tarfon says: It shall be given to the one who is under the greatest disadvantage. Rabbi Akiva says: We do not show mercy in a matter of law.

As the continuation shows, Akiva had quite different halakic reasons, which we will ignore here.[82] In any case he was wrong. Whether on the surface, below the surface, or triggered by the surface of the text within its recipients and interpreters, emotions come along with law, influence it, are reflected by it, complicate it, and become part of its rhetorical advancement.

Status Infringements and Hierarchical Structures

Whether or not various sexual behaviours and strategies for acquiring resources are understood as functional or dysfunctional, largely depends on the hierarchical social structures they are embedded in. Hierarchy, too, evolved because it had certain adaptive advantages, especially as human societies grew larger and more complex, sedentary, and specialised. Interaction could no longer depend on close personal relationships only, as in small hunter-gatherer bands, but also on rumour and

---

[82] This is also an issue of the impartiality of the legal process versus empathic concerns.

reputation for skill, strength, influence, and reliability, which translate to position, status, rank, and honour.[83]

The effects are somewhat paradoxical. Human views of what is unacceptable or dysfunctional with regard to sexual or property infringements – as well as other types of interpersonal infringements – are relative to the dominant hierarchical structures. Laws emerge that reflect emotional reactions to various infringements, balance them against each other, and regulate and domesticate some of the exaggerations that instinct-driven reactions would lead to. All of this takes place, however, within current social hierarchies. In a hierarchical context, to kill or rape subordinates would be considered less of a crime than the opposite, even less than for a male slave to engage in voluntary sex with his master's wife[84] or for a low-status person to challenge someone higher up on the ladder, with or without violence. Similarly, it would often be considered worse for a subordinate to cheat or steal from a superior, and especially from a temple,[85] than for a high-ranking person to acquire or expropriate resources from the lower classes.

Perhaps one could say that within a hierarchical context, breaches of hierarchy itself, or infringements on status and honour, constitute the ultimate infringement, under which sexual, property, and all other infringements can be subsumed. Worst are disloyalty and breaches in patron-client relationships, whether as a slave towards a master, as a vassal people against one's overlord, or as in the case of Israel's relationship to Yahweh.

> They abandoned the Lord, and worshipped Baal and the Astartes. So the anger of the Lord was kindled against Israel, and he gave them over to plunderers who plundered them, and he sold them into the power of their enemies all around, so that they could no longer withstand their enemies. ... So the anger of the Lord was kindled against Israel; and he said, "Because this people have transgressed my covenant that I commanded their ancestors, and have not obeyed my voice, I will no longer drive out before them any of the nations that Joshua left when he died" (Judg 2:13–14, 20–21 NRSV).

In this representation of the relationship between a people and their ultimate overlord, divine anger (אַף יְהוָה) is directed towards those who do not submit to and acknowledge their god's supremacy (SIZE) and thereby infringe upon his status. Whether the penalty is proportionate in relation to the infringement (MEASURE)

---

[83] Kent Flannery and Joyce Marcus, *The Creation of Inequality: How Our Prehistoric Ancestors Set the Stage for Monarchy, Slavery, and Empire* (Cambridge, MA: Harvard University Press, 2012).

[84] One of the first to point out the inconsistency and double standards in such behaviour was probably the Stoic philosopher Musonius Rufus (*Musonius Rufus* 12).

[85] See LH 8, for one example among many.

is not an issue since the relationship is highly asymmetric. There is divine pity, too
(יְהוָה יִנָּחֵם Judg 2:18), in response to the crying people (מִנַּאֲקָתָם Judg 2:18), but it
is effectively constrained by their lack of loyalty and submission.[86] Deuterono-
mistic texts reflecting the notion of covenant treaty circumscribe human infringements on divine status, but unlike laws relating to interhuman infringements, they
contain few or no restrictions against excessive responses from the superior party.
There is no higher authority to keep divine anger in check.[87]

In cases of interpersonal infringement, hierarchies (SIZE) define justice (MEAS-
URE), too, but we find a certain balance between the two frameworks – even
though it is often asymmetric. As we have seen in the foregoing discussions of sexual and property infringements, considerations of justice depend on relative status
and sometimes stand in tension with the hierarchical framework in which they are
embedded. For example, an infringement from an approximately equal male on
another male is seen as causing shame of a kind that elicits strong response and
retaliation, while the emotion of shame instilled in a woman subjected to the *sotah*
ritual is inarticulate and shaming her is a prerogative of her superiors, fixing her in
the subordinate position in which she is thought to belong.[88] Infringements on
equals and their revenge are regulated and circumscribed, as are infringements on
subordinates and dependents in some cases – they are at least frowned upon, and
infringements on superiors are strongly avenged.

The latter type of response is modified as ideals of rationality, mental strength,
and emotional self-control become influential, as they do in particular during the
Hellenistic and Roman periods, not least under Stoic influence.[89] High-status

---

[86] Cf. also Jer 11:10–11 (NRSV), where God says he will not listen when the people cry (וְזָעֲקוּ):
"They have turned back to the iniquities of their ancestors of old, who refused to heed my words;
they have gone after other gods to serve them; the house of Israel and the house of Judah have
broken the covenant that I made with their ancestors. Therefore, thus says the Lord, assuredly I
am going to bring disaster upon them that they cannot escape; though they cry out to me, I will
not listen to them."

[87] Cf. the curses and threats in Deut 28–29.

[88] For shame and subordination, see Kazen, "Viewing Oneself," also in this volume.

[89] Konstan, *Before Forgiveness: The Origins of a Moral Idea* (Cambridge: Cambridge University Press, 2010), 23–37; idem, "Assuaging Rage: Remorse, Repentance, and Forgiveness in the
Classical World," in *Ancient Forgiveness: Classical, Judaic, and Christian* (ed. Charles L. Griswold and David Konstan; Cambridge: Cambridge University Press, 2012), 17–30 (17–21). In *Rhetoric*, Aristotle sees anger (ὀργή) as a reaction to pain in the sense of goal blockages and disappoint-
ments, specifically as a reaction to an inappropriate status infringement (*Rhet.* 2.2. 1378a–1380a).
The context is competitive and hierarchical: an infringement requires compensation to restore

individuals are increasingly expected to act with modest restraint and neither act on their immediate desires, nor defend their honour excessively. In fact, an aristocrat's response to status infringements, at least from an inferior, is to ignore it. Only when an infringement really threatens one's position is there reason to retaliate. Hierarchy still defines infringements, but responses to status infringements partly change in character. Examples are found in the Torah reception and interpretation of Jewish Hellenistic literature, such as Sirach, as well as the hypothetical sayings source Q, which was incorporated into the gospel tradition. This, however, is part of a larger story for which there is no room here.[90]

Conclusion

So, what have we learnt? Human behaviour is very much governed by emotions that depend on our social and bodily experiences, as well as on the conceptual metaphors we associate with these experiences and with our understanding of morality and moral infringements. The metaphors MEASURE and SIZE have been seen relating to experiences and emotions that are crucial for justice, integrity, honour, status, revenge, and compensation. Law circumscribes infringements, resulting from behaviours often triggered by emotions related to the metaphorical frame of

---

the social position of the wronged party. "Anger is precisely the desire to adjust the record in this way," says Konstan (*The Emotions of the Ancient Greeks: Studies in Aristotle and Classical Literature* [The Robson Classical Lectures; Toronto: University of Toronto Press, 2006], 75). Aristotle's great-souled man (μεγαλόψυχός) in *Nicomachean Ethics* 4.3 is concerned with honours but shows a relative indifference and overlooks wrongs rather than bears a grudge (*Eth. nic.* 1124a). The basis for such behaviour is a sense of superiority and a "perfectionist ethical scheme" (Charles L. Griswold, *Forgiveness: A Philosophical Exploration* [Cambridge: Cambridge University Press, 2007], 7–9). Griswold (*Forgiveness*, 10–12) finds Plato even more extreme in this regard: a virtuous person like Socrates cannot be harmed and cannot be moved to anger (*Apol.* 30c–d; 41d). The Stoic sage is similarly supposed to be invulnerable to infringements and hence would feel no resentment or need no revenge (Griswold, *Forgiveness*, 12–13). Anger is not fitting for him. Seneca finds anger eager for revenge, not caring about the consequences, and bringing down the avenger simultaneously (*Ira* 1.1.1). In Seneca's view, anger is useless for revenge (*Ira* 1.12.5) and reason rather speaks for overlooking infringements (*Ira* 2.14.3). To forego revenge is simply a sign of superiority, indicating that one considers the offender insignificant and unworthy, like an unwitting animal (*Ira* 2.32–33). Musonius Rufus (10) goes even further, arguing that a wise man will not prosecute anyone for personal status infringements (ὕβρεως), since he does not consider himself insulted. The good man simply cannot be injured by the bad.

   [90] Cf. Thomas Kazen, "Altruism and Prosocial Ideals in the Sermon: Between Human Nature and Divine Potential," in *Social and Cognitive Perspectives on the Sermon on the Mount* (ed. Rikard Roitto, Colleen Shantz, and Petri Luomanen; Sheffield: Equinox, 2021), 82–109. See also idem, "Self-Preserving and Other-Oriented Concerns"; "Emotional Ethics," also in this volume.

SIZE, which were once – at some stage in evolutionary history – adaptive, but have partly and increasingly become dysfunctional within the complex social structures and networks of human society. Law also effects moral repair by drawing on other, similarly adaptive emotions, related to the MEASURE frame, and intent on facilitating social interaction and cooperation.

With the help of a fair measure of reduction, these complex relationships could perhaps be illustrated with the following figure:

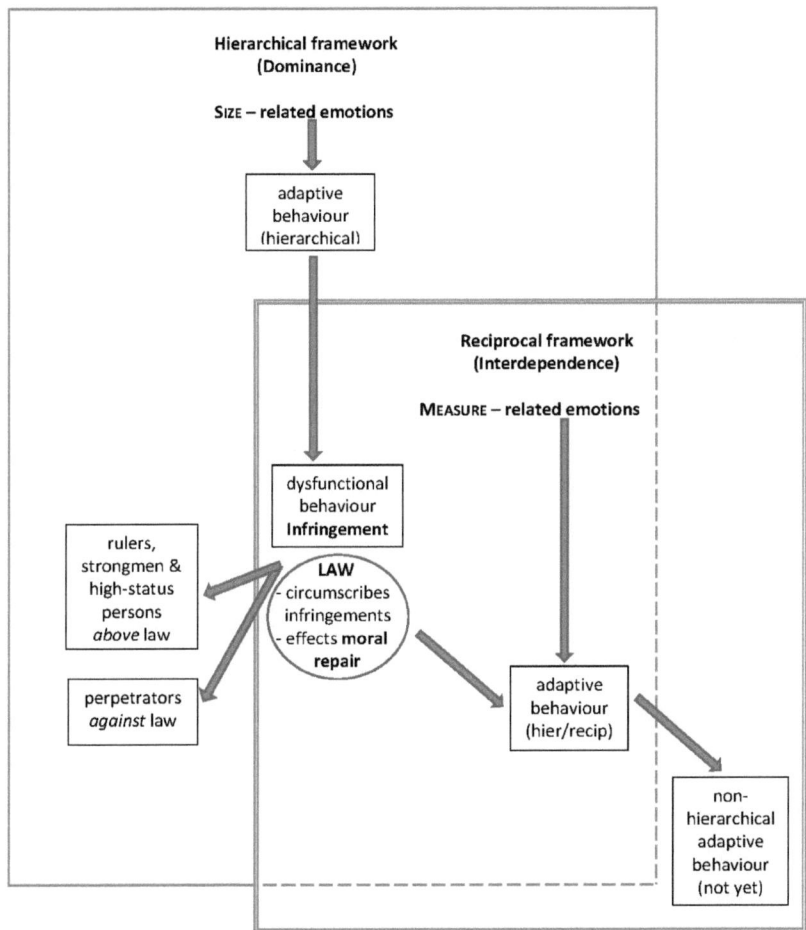

Figure 1

Behaviour that might have been originally adaptive within an entirely hierarchical framework and driven by SIZE-related emotions, becomes increasingly dysfunctional and experienced as infringements within a markedly reciprocal framework, in which MEASURE-related emotions play a greater role for human interactions. Law has the function of circumscribing such infringements and effect moral repair, advocating a different behaviour, more adapted to a context of social interdependence, but simultaneously remaining within a relatively hierarchical framework. Rulers, strongmen, and certain other high-status persons often operate above the law, as if they were (partly) independent of ordinary social networks, and perpetrators somewhat similarly act beside or against the law.

In theory, we could conceive of a radically non-hierarchical behaviour being adaptive within a markedly reciprocal framework, but outside of a strictly hierarchical framework. Such a context – and hence, such behaviour – is, however, not (yet) conceptualised in the world of the ancient sources we have examined and is, sadly to say, rarely to be found today either.

Acknowledgement: The research for this article was funded by the Swedish Research Council, grant nr. 2016-02319.

Retribution and Repair in Voluntary Associations

Comparing Rule Texts from Qumran, Collegia, *and Christ Groups*

Introduction

In the ancient world, like today, people solved their conflicts around norm infringements at different levels. The household was, of course, the most basic social sphere, governed in a patriarchal world by the *paterfamilias*. Outside of the family, hierarchical relationships and power structures would govern who had the right to adjudicate in cases of conflict and on whose terms decisions would be made. In societies with well-organised social structures, judicial systems of one or another sort were often involved in the moral repair of interpersonal infringements. In larger societies, however, various subgroups were often able to administer their own justice, keep their own control, and mete out their own sanctions. Between the household or clan and the village or city, there was a space in which associations of various kind could operate.[1] We know of such associations or *collegia* mainly from the Hellenistic and Roman periods, and the ways in which they organised and viewed themselves were largely inspired by the structure and function of civic authorities, which they frequently seem to have emulated.[2]

---

[1] See John S. Kloppenborg and Richard S. Ascough, *Greco-Roman Associations: Texts, Translations, and Commentary*, vol. 1: *Attica, Central Greece, Macedonia, Thrace* (BZNW 181; Berlin: De Gruyter, 2011), 1.

[2] This point is regularly indicated through the history of association research, e.g., Edwin Hatch, *The Organisation of the Early Christian Churches: Eight Lectures Delivered before the University of Oxford, in the Year 1880* (Bampton Lectures; London: Rivingtons, 1881); Edwin A. Judge, *The Social Pattern of the Christian Groups in the First Century: Some Prolegomena to the*

Associations were of different kinds, ranging from vocational to religious to ethnic.[3] They served the mutual benefit of their members in the multi-faceted, fragmented, and culturally diverse social contexts of the Roman empire. During recent decades, the study of Greek and Roman associations has informed our analysis of early Jewish and Christ-believing groups, so that we now tend to see these as a subspecies of ancient *collegia*.[4]

Comparison between different groups is interesting in several areas. For my purposes, it is relevant to explore and compare ways in which moral infringements, in particular interpersonal infringements, were handled. One of the functions of ancient associations was to regulate retribution and repair of norm infringements within the limits of the group, in order to keep the group together. This perspective opens up new possibilities to analyse and interpret group interaction in such communities, and to compare their attitudes and strategies to norm infringement and moral repair.

In the present article I will analyse and compare ideas, practices, and rituals for the repair of interpersonal moral infringements in association laws, rule texts, and early Christian texts that attempt to regulate life in congregations of early Christ-believers, for example as expressed in Pauline paraenesis. What are the goals and

---

Study of New Testament Ideas of Social Obligation (London: Tyndale Press, 1960); Moshe Weinfeld, *The Organizational Pattern and the Penal Code of the Qumran Sect: A Comparison with Guilds and Religious Associations of the Hellenistic-Roman Period* (Novum Testamentum Et Orbis Antiquus 2; Fribourg: Editions Universitaires Fribourg Suisse), 1986; and especially Yonder Moynihan Gillihan, *Civic Ideology, Organization, and Law in the Rule Scrolls: A Comparative Study of the Covenanters' Sect and Contemporary Voluntary Associations in Political Context* (STDJ 97; Leiden: Brill, 2012). Kloppenborg points out that Roman associations were usually organised along patterns of the city and the army, while Greek associations were more varied (John S. Kloppenborg, "Collegia and *Thiasoi*: Issues in Function, Taxonomy and Membership," in *Voluntary Associations in the Graeco-Roman World* (ed. John S. Kloppenborg and Stephen G. Wilson; London: Routledge, 1996), 16–30. Kloppenborg and Ascough talk of "mimicry of the *polis*" (*Greco-Roman Associations*, vol. 1, 6). Gillihan argues that "the Covenanters' civic ideology was a rather direct response to Hasmonean state civic ideology" (*Civic Ideology*, xvii).

[3] For overviews of various types of ancient associations, see Kloppenborg and Ascough, *Greco-Roman Associations*, 1–3; Philip A. Harland, *Dynamics of Identity in the World of the Early Christians: Associations, Judeans, and Cultural Minorities* (New York: T & T Clark, 2009), 32–35; idem, *Associations, Synagogues, and Congregations: Claiming a Place in Ancient Mediterranean Society*, 2nd ed. (http://philipharland.com/publications/Harland%202013%20Associations-Synagogues-Congregations.pdf, 2013), 19–43.

[4] Admittedly, the image of subspecies has one major disadvantage: it easily conjures up notions of genetic relationship and development. To some extent this applies to notions such as family resemblance, too. While scholars in the past often thought in terms of genealogy, we should rather think in terms of analogy. Cf. Harland, *Dynamics of Identity*, 161–185.

effects of these mechanisms of retribution and repair? What roles do hierarchy and honour play in these particular contexts? Can we gain further insights by looking at associations as trust networks, and by applying commitment (or costly) signalling theory, game theory (reputation), and the valuable relationships hypothesis?

A Short Research History

Comparative research relating to associations goes back to the 19th century, with Georg Heinrici and Edwin Hatch as prominent figures, to some degree prefigured by Theodor Mommsen.[5] They had little following, however, as many biblical scholars were hesitant for ideological reasons to pursue analogies between Greco-Roman associations and early Christian communities.[6] Edwin Judge in a sense

---

[5] Georg Heinrici, "Zum genossenschaftlichen Charakter der paulinischen Christengemeinden" *Theologische Studien und Kritiken* 54 (1881): 505–524; Hatch, *Organization*; Theodor Mommsen, *De collegiis et sodaliciis Romanorum; Accedit inscriptio Lanuvina* (Kiliae: Libraaria Schwersiana, 1843). For research histories, beginning with these 19th-century roots of association research, see Harland, *Associations, Synagogues, and Congregations*, 162–166; Thomas Schmeller, "Zum exegetischen Interesse an antiken Vereinen im 19. und 20. Jahrhundert," in *Vereine, Synagogen und Gemeinden im kaiserzeitlichen Kleinasien* (ed. Andreas Gutsfeld and Dietrich-Alex Koch; STAC; Tübingen: Mohr Siebeck, 2006), 1–19. Cf. Richard S. Ascough, "Voluntary Associations and the Formation of Pauline Christian Communities: Overcoming the Objections," in *Vereine, Synagogen und Gemeinden* (ed. Gutsfeld and Koch), 151–153; Kloppenborg and Ascough, *Greco-Roman Associations*, vol. 1, 209–210. For comprehensive research histories of associations in general, see Margret Dissen, *Römische Kollegien und Deutsche Geschichtswissenschaft im 19. und 20. Jahrhundert* (Stuttgart: Steiner, 2009); and Jonathan S. Perry, *The Roman Collegia: The Modern Evolution of an Ancient Concept* (Leiden: Brill, 2006). Recent contributions to association research include Christian Thomsen, *The Politics of Association in Hellenistic Rhodes* (Edinburgh: Edinburgh University Press, 2020); Benedikt Eckhardt, *Romanisierung und Verbrüderung: Das Vereinswesen im römischen Reich* (BAG 34; Berlin: De Gruyter, 2021); Przemysław Wojciechowski, *Roman Religious Associations in Italy (1st–3rd century)* (Toruń: Nicolaus Copernicus University Press, 2021); and the collection of essays edited by Vincent Gabrielsen and Mario C. D. Paganini, *Private Associations in the Ancient Greek World: Regulations and the Creation of Group Identity* (Cambridge: Cambridge University Press, 2021). For a comprehensive bibliography on association research, see John S. Kloppenborg, "Associations in the Greco-Roman World, in *Oxford Bibliographies* online, 2016 (DOI: 10.1093/OBO/9780195393361-0064), and Harland's ongoing and updated bibliography at http://philipharland.com/greco-roman-associations/welcome/bibliography-on-associations-in-the-greco-roman-world/ (viewed 8 March 2022).

[6] See the discussion in John S. Kloppenborg, "Greco-Roman *Thiasoi*, the *Ekklēsia* at Corinth, and Conflict Management," in *Redescribing Paul and the Corinthians* (Early Christianity and Its Literature 5; ed. Ron Cameron and Merrill P. Miller; Atlanta, GA: Society of Biblical

reopened the topic in 1960, although the significance of this aspect of his work was not immediately recognised by scholars of early Christianity.[7] There is still a tendency in some quarters to downplay such analogies in favour of views that emphasise the unique character and organisation of Christ-believing groups.[8]

At about the same time as Judge renewed comparisons between congregations and associations, Qumran scholars seem to have realised the potential of analogy with voluntary associations, especially in regard to rule texts. The first to compare D (the Damascus Document) and S (the Community Rule – *Serekh ha-Yaḥad*) with Greco-Roman association rules was probably Hans Bardtke, beginning in 1961,[9] and a few other scholars followed suit. Moshe Weinfeld published a brief but pregnant monograph in 1986,[10] which became a standard work on the matter. It contains comparative examples from seventeen association rules, including translations of the inscription of the *nomos* of the Athenian *Iobakchoi* (a Dionysiac *nomos*), an inscription from the Ein-Gedi synagogue, and the pseudo-Clementine epistle of Peter to James. Weinfeld suggests that Greco-Roman associations influenced the organisation and rules of the sectarians reflected in D and S. Especially the penalties and fines show that the sectarians and other Greco-Roman associations are groups of a similar type.[11] Based on this, Weinfeld argues against Lawrence Schiffman that the rules are not essentially based on scriptural interpretation and halakic activity.[12]

Since then, a handful of Qumran scholars have addressed the issue in brief studies, from different angles, arguing everything from Jewish and no Hellenistic influence, to Pythagorean influence. Yonder Moynihan Gillihan provides a comprehensive history of comparative research in his 2012 monograph on civic

---

Literature, 2011), 187–218, including a criticism also of Wayne Meeks, *The First Urban Christians: The Social World of the Apostle Paul* (New Haven, CT: Yale University Press, 1983), for overemphasising differences, but later acknowledging the progress made in association research. For analogies, cf. also idem, "Associations, Christ Groups, and Their Place in the Polis," *Zeitschrift für die neutestamentliche Wissenschaft* 108.1 (2017), 1–56; and already idem, "Collegia and *Thiasoi*."

[7] Judge, "Social Pattern"; cf. Harland, *Associations, Synagogues, and Congregations*, 163.

[8] Cf. the discussion in Harland, *Associations, Synagogues, and Congregations*, 164–167.

[9] Hans Bardtke, "Die Rechtsstellung der Qumrān-Gemeinde," *Theologische Literaturzeitung* 86 (1961), 93–104. For a discussion, see Gillihan, *Civic Ideology*, 37–41.

[10] Weinfeld, *Organizational Pattern*.

[11] Ibid., 23–43.

[12] Ibid., 71–76. Cf. Lawrence H. Schiffman, *Sectarian Law in the Dead Sea Scrolls: Courts, Testimony, and the Penal Code* (BJS 33; Chico, CA: Scholars Press, 1983).

ideology, organization and law in the rule scrolls.[13] Gillihan, whose study is by far the largest and most detailed on the issue so far, argues that voluntary associations claimed authority typically reserved for the state and that the organisation of the covenanters expresses an alternative civic ideology, which could either be in response or opposition to the ruling order, or analogous and complementary. Gillihan carries out a detailed comparison with Epicureans, Stoics, Cynics, the Pauline congregations, and Roman plebs.[14]

Comparison between association texts and the New Testament, especially Paul, did not receive much attention until the 1980s. From that time onwards, a number of important studies have appeared, some of which find their inspiration from a reading seminar at the University of Toronto, beginning in the 1990s,[15] such as the works of Richard Ascough, Philip Harland, and John Kloppenborg, variously focusing on Macedonia and Asia Minor.[16] Several scholars outside of the English language area have also published recent studies relating early Christ-

---

[13] Gillihan, *Civic Ideology*, 37–64. For more recent contributions, see for example Andrew R. Krause, "Qumran Discipline and Rites of Affliction in Their Associational Context," in *Private Associations and Jewish Communities in the Hellenistic and Roman Cities* (ed. Benedikt Eckhardt; SupJSJ 191; Leiden: Brill, 2019), 58–75.

[14] Gillihan, *Civic Ideology*, 505–513 provides a helpful summary.

[15] See Kloppenborg and Ascough, *Greco-Roman Associations*, vol. 1, v–viii.

[16] Richard S. Ascough, *Paul's Macedonian Associations: The Social Context of Philippians and 1 Thessalonians* (WUNT 2.61; Tübingen: Mohr Siebeck, 2003); idem, "Voluntary Associations and the Formation of Pauline Christian Communities"; idem, "The Apostolic Decree of Acts and Greco-Roman Associations: Eating in the Shadow of the Roman Empire," in *Aposteldekret und antike Vereinswesen: Gemeinschaft und ihre Ordnung* (ed. Markus Öhler; WUNT 280; Tübingen: Mohr Siebeck, 2011), 297–316; idem, "What Are They Now Saying about Christ Groups and Associations," *Currents in Biblical Research* 13.2 (2015): 207–244; Harland, *Dynamics of Identity*; idem, *Associations, Synagogues, and Congregations*; Kloppenborg, "Collegia and *Thiasoi*"; idem, "Associations in the Ancient World," in *The Historical Jesus in His Context* (ed. Amy-Jill Levine, Dale C. Allison Jr., and John Dominic Crossan; Princeton Readings in Religion; Princeton, NJ: Princeton University Press, 2006), 323–338; idem, "Associations, Voluntary," in *Encyclopedia of the Bible and Its Reception*, vol. 2 (ed. Constance M. Furey, et al.; Berlin: De Gruyter, 2009), 1062–1069; idem, *Christ's Associations: Connecting and Belonging in the Ancient City* (New Haven, CT: Yale University Press, 2019). This group of scholars are also producing a multi-volume collection of the most important association inscriptions, organised regionally. Three of the volumes have appeared so far: Kloppenborg and Ascough, *Greco-Roman Associations*, vol 1 (*GRA* I); Philipp Harland, *Greco-Roman Associations: Texts, Translations, and Commentary*, vol 2: *North Coast of the Black Sea, Asia Minor* (BZNW 204; Berlin: De Gruyter, 2014) (*GRA* II); and John S. Kloppenborg, *Greco-Roman Associations: Texts, Translations, and Commentary*, vol. 3: *Ptolemaic and Early Roman Egypt* (BZNW 246; Berlin: De Gruyter, 2020) (*GRA* III).

believing communities to Greco-Roman association, for example Eva Ebel's study on associations and Paul's first letter to the Corinthians, and Markus Öhler's discussions of Christ-groups in Judea and in the Book of Acts.[17] Today there are more people taking part in what could be described as an increasing trend to draw on association research in interpretations of New Testament texts and the social and political lives of early Christ-believers.

In line with this trend, the choice between looking for analogies with early Christ-groups either in associations or in synagogues has become somewhat unnatural. While the synagogue had often previously been seen as an alternative background for early Christian congregations, synagogues themselves came to be compared to Greco-Roman associations and studied in the light of, or in analogy with, such groups, especially with regard to their organisation and their practices.[18] Diaspora synagogues in particular have been compared to associations and similarities have been observed between their systems of benefaction.[19] Some scholars suggest that we differentiate between synagogues as public, communal meetings or

---

[17] Eva Ebel, *Die Attraktivität früher christlicher Gemeinden: Die Gemeinde von Korinth im Spiegel griechisch-römischer Vereine* (WUNT 2.178; Tübingen: Mohr Siebeck, 2004); Markus Öhler, "Römisches Vereinsrecht und christliche Gemeinden," in *Zwischen den Reichen: Neues Testament und Römische Herrschaft* (ed. Michael Labahn and Jürgen Zangenberg; Tübingen: Francke, 2002), 51–71; idem, "Die Jerusalemer Urgemeinde im Spiegel des antiken Vereinswesens," *New Testament Studies* 51 (2005): 393–415. See also various articles in *Religiöse Vereine in der römischen Antike Untersuchungen zu Organisation, Ritual und Raumordnung* (ed. Ulrike Egelhaaf-Geiser and Alfred Schäfer; STAC 13; Tübingen: Mohr Siebeck, 2002); *Vereine, Synagogen und Gemeinden* (ed. Gutsfeld and Koch); *Aposteldekret und antikes Vereinswesen: Gemeinschaft und ihre Ordnung* (ed. Markus Öhler; WUNT 280; Tübingen: Mohr Siebeck, 2011); Benedikt Eckhardt and Clemens Leonhard, *Juden, Christen und Vereine im Römischen Reich: Mit einem Beitrag von Philip A. Harland* (Religionsgeschichtliche Versuche und Vorarbeiten 75; Berlin: De Gruyter, 2018); *Authority and Identity in Emerging Christianities in Asia Minor and Greece* (ed. Cilliers Breytenbach and Julien M. Ogereau; AJEC 103; Leiden: Brill, 2018).

[18] Harland, *Associations, Synagogues, and Congregations.* Cf. also Martin Hengel "Proseuche und Synagoge: Jüdische Gemeinde, Gotteshaus und Gottesdienst in der Diaspora und in Palästina," in *Tradition und Glaube: Das frühe Christentum in seiner Umwelt* (ed. Gert Jeremias, Heinz-Wolfgang Kuhn, and Hartmut Stegemann; Göttingen: Vandenhoeck & Ruprecht, 1971), 157–184; and Peter Richardson, *Building Jewish in the Roman East* (Waco, TX: Baylor, 2004).

[19] Harland, *Associations, Synagogues, and Congregations.* For a short overview of topics in synagogue research and how they relate to understanding synagogues as associations, see Anders Runesson, Donald D. Binder, and Birger Olsson, *The Ancient Synagogue from Its Origins to 200 C.E.: A Source Book* (Leiden: Brill, 2008), 7–13.

meeting places, as was mostly the case in the land of Israel, and diaspora synagogues as Jewish voluntary associations.[20]

Theoretical Perspectives

Against this background of previous research, I think that analysis and comparison could be enhanced by some sociocognitive and psychological theories and by perspectives from evolutionary science. To some extent, association research has already entered social-scientific territory by using social network analysis.[21] Kloppenborg, in particular, has in several contexts discussed associations in relation to network theory, including structure, network intersection, and the role of so-called weak links, or weak ties.[22] Social network theory thus helps us to understand and explain the spread and influence of ideas and practices within and between groups.

Network theory can be used in a number of contexts. Charles Tilly has developed certain aspects of network analysis in his 2005 book *Trust and Rule*. He defines a *trust network* as a network of strong ties, which "gives one member significant claims on the attention or aid of another" and in which members "are collectively carrying on major long-term enterprises such as procreation, long-distance trade, workers' mutual aid or practice of an underground religion." The character of the ties "sets the collective enterprise at risk to the malfeasance, mistakes, and failures of individual members."[23] Trust networks include anything from religious sects to trade networks, or patron-client chains. One of Tilly's points is the

---

[20] Anders Runesson, *The Origins of the Synagogue: A Socio-Historical Study* (ConBNT 37; Stockholm: Almqvist & Wiksell International, 2001). The distinction between public synagogues and association synagogues (which to some extent also existed in the Land of Israel) has subsequently been taken up by others. Cf. Jordan J. Ryan, *The Role of the Synagogue in the Aims of Jesus* (Minneapolis, MN: Fortress, 2017); Andrew R. Krause, *Synagogues in the Works of Flavius Josephus: Rhetoric, Spatiality, and First-Century Jewish Institutions* (AJEC 97; Leiden: Brill, 2017).

[21] Social network analysis was developed in mathematical sociology, particularly from the 1940s and onwards, but with older roots. It is associated with names such as Anatol Rapoport, Mark Granovetter, and Barry Wellman.

[22] Kloppenborg, *Christ's Associations*; idem, "Recruitment to Elective Cults: Network Structure and Ecology," *New Testament Studies* 66.2 (2020): 323–335. Cf. István Czachesz, "Women, Charity, and Mobility in early Christianity: Weak Links and the Historical Transformation of religions," In *Changing Minds: Religion and Cognition through the Ages* (ed. István Czachesz and Tamás Biró; Leuven: Peeters, 2011), 129–154.

[23] Charles Tilly, *Trust and Rule* (Cambridge Studies in Comparative Politics; Cambridge: Cambridge University Press, 2005), 4.

relationship between such networks and the political rulers or the political system; they often constitute an alternative, or at least a complement, to the social and political organisation. Although placing one's resources at risk is one of the characteristics of a trust network, people are part of such relationships precisely to protect themselves against risk and increase control. The price is often conformity and trust networks are often hierarchic. Ties within trust networks are thick and last long.[24] These are reasons why trust networks, rather than cities or states, have often "formed the social basis for most weighty, high-risk, long-term collective enterprises."[25]

In a short study of Ptolemaic religious associations, from 2006, Andrew Monson applies Tilly's model to association research and shows how associations in antiquity functioned as trust networks, in which people invested and put their resources at risk. They did this in order to "lower the costs of cooperation, enabling associations to ensure members of a proper burial and protect them from economic or legal catastrophes."[26] Costly investments and adherence to the society's rules signal commitment to others and build trust and confidence. Fines and punishments on the other hand keep less serious people away or push them out. This strengthens the trust network and distinguishes it from other social networks, by making cooperation within it less costly.[27]

Monson argues, however, that economic incentives are only part of the explanation and emphasises the role of social relations. The written rules "transform informal norms shared by the group into institutions that constrain behavior," so that norms that distinguish trust networks from other social networks become institutionalised.[28] As part of this picture, associations generally want to solve their disputes internally, and "protect their local networks of trust against intrusion from state officials."[29] As Tilly points out, trust networks in certain regards stand in some tension with the central power and in other regards there is mutual dependence. The relationship between trust networks and rulers or governments is

---

[24] Tilly, *Trust and Rule*, 1–29, 43–51.

[25] Tilly, "Cities, States, and Trust Networks: Chapter 1 of Cities and States in World History," *Theory and Society* 39.3–4 (2010): 265–280 (272).

[26] Andrew Monson, "The Ethics and Economics of Ptolemaic Religious Associations," *Ancient Society* 36 (2006), 221–238 (237).

[27] Ibid., 237.

[28] Ibid., 233–234, 238 (quotation from 234).

[29] Ibid., 235–238 (quotation from 237–238).

complex: they can both compete and complement; they can be anything from exploited to suppressed by the central power.[30]

The emphasis on putting resources at risk within a context of thick social relationships, in order to lower the costs of cooperation, has clear affinities to evolutionary and psychobiological models, such as the *costly*, or *commitment signalling theory*.[31] Certain behaviours that on the surface seem costly to the individual, may have adaptive advantages by providing better mating opportunities, enhancing status, indicating honesty, seriousness, and strength, and creating trust and reputation. To simplify: delayed benefits exceed the immediate costs. Costly signalling theory can be employed to explain many animal and human behaviours, from risk taking to religious rituals.[32]

Costly or commitment signalling theory suggests that we often engage in personally disadvantageous behaviour, including elaborate and painstaking rituals, because of the goodwill and confidence we receive from the community. Faithful observance of hard-to-fake signals proves that one is not a cheater or a free rider, but a trustworthy person, prepared to invest in common concerns.[33] Membership requirements, fees, fines, and subordination under strict codes or rules of conduct count among such costly signals that inspire confidence and enhance reputation. Systems built on commitment signalling are to some extent self-regulating: long-term benefits overbalance the costs when you signal commitment, but costs overbalance benefits for those who cheat.

Commitment signalling theory partly draws on, or relates to, *game theory*, another evolutionary and psychobiological approach, which is also based on

---

[30] Tilly, *Trust and Rule*, 50–51; idem, "Cities, States, and Trust Networks."

[31] Costly signalling theory developed from Amotz Zahavi's idea of a selection for handicap in mate selection. Amotz Zahavi, "Mate Selection: A Selection for a Handicap," *Journal of Theoretical Biology* 54 (1975). For overviews, see Rebecca Bliege Bird and Eric Alden Smith, "Signaling Theory, Strategic Interaction, and Symbolic Capital," *Current Anthropology* 46/2 (2005), 221–248; Francis T. McAndrew, "Costly Signaling Theory," in *Encyclopedia of Evolutionary Psychological Science* (ed. Todd K. Shackelford and Viviana A. Weekes-Shackelford; Cham: Springer, 2019).

[32] Cf. articles in *Evolution and the Capacity for Commitment* (ed. Randolph M. Nesse; New York: Russel Sage Foundation, 2001).

[33] For an application of costly signalling theory to religion and religious cooperation in particular, see William Irons, "Religion as a Hard-to-Fake Sign of Commitment," in *Evolution and the Capacity for Commitment* (ed. Nesse), 292–309; Joseph Bulbulia, "Charismatic Signalling," *Journal for the Study of Religion, Nature and Culture* 3.4 (2009), 518–551; Joseph Bulbulia and Richard Sosis, "Signalling Theory and the Evolution of Religious Cooperation," *Religion* 41.3 (2011).

economics and mathematics. As human instincts evolved in small-scale societies, interactions were not anonymous, and reputation crucial for success, that is, reputation had an adaptive value.[34] From an evolutionary perspective, cooperation was necessary for survival in the past, and continues to be so for success in an evolving world of increasingly complex social webs.

Game theory illustrates the intricate balancing acts that are often required. In "the prisoner's dilemma," the payoff is high for the one who defects if the other cooperates, moderate when both cooperate, and low when both defect. In one-shot games, people usually try to maximise their own gain, but as soon as games are played in several rounds, players quickly learn to cooperate. Repeated defections are usually punished by reciprocal defections, but then forgiven if, sometimes even before, the other player resumes cooperation. Maybe it was a mistake![35]

For the equation to work, people need to experience a reasonable degree of fairness. The "ultimatum game," shows that many people prefer to receive no gain, rather than being treated too unfairly.[36] From an evolutionary point of view, the human species is social because it makes for survival. Each member benefits from others by contributing. But within the system, hierarchy governs the distribution of benefits and honour. As we will see, associations were hierarchical fellowships,

---

[34] Johan Almenberg and Anna Dreber, "Economics and Evolution: Complementary Perspectives on Cooperation," in *Evolution, Games, and God: The Principle of Cooperation* (ed. Martin A. Nowak and Sarah Coakley; Cambridge, MA: Harvard University Press, 2013): 132–149.

[35] For a (perhaps *the*) classic study of game theory, with a theoretical, mathematical perspective, see Herbert Gintis, *Game Theory Evolving: A Problem-Centered Introduction to Modeling Strategic Interaction*, 2nd ed. (Princeton, NJ: Princeton University Press, 2009). For a similarly classic study of slightly more "applied" character, see Robert Axelrod, *The Evolution of Cooperation*, rev. ed. (Cambridge, MA: Basic Books, 2006). For game theory in relation to experimental real-life studies, see for example Colin F. Camerer, *Behavioral Game Theory: Experiments in Strategic Interaction* (New York: Russel Sage Foundation; Princeton, NJ: Princeton University Press, 2003).

[36] This is clear from numerous experimental studies. Camerer points out that experimental data addresses two important criticisms of mathematical game theory: "first, that game theory assumes more calculation, foresight, perceived rationality of others, and (in empirical applications) self-interest than most people are naturally capable of; and, second, that in most applied domains there is too much theorizing about how rational people would interact strategically, relative to the modest amount of empirical evidence on how they do interact" (Camerer, *Behavioral Game Theory*, 465). Models predict behaviour, but "behavioural game theory" modifies models with experimental evidence.

which also fits with their classification as trust networks. Fairness is expected, but within a markedly hierarchical framework.[37]

The tension between justice and domination is complicated. Hierarchy inspires competition for honour and status, which invites conflict and may lead to interpersonal infringements and abuse. This, in turn, evokes an urge for revenge, which counteracts the character and damages the purpose of a voluntary association, namely conformity and cooperation. Hierarchy paradoxically has to suppress what it evokes and counter the urge for revenge, while inspiring a legitimate striving for status. This requires a volatile balance between inequality and control, which can be seen in many association texts.

To protect one's honour by taking revenge *within* one's group becomes highly dysfunctional from the perspective of the larger group and its need for cooperation and loyalty. It benefits everyone to restrict conflicts within the group. It saves resources and keeps the group together, reinforcing mutual dependence, in spite of a hierarchical order. Revenge also becomes problematic for the individual, who is in dire need of the group's support. The *valuable relationships theory* suggests, based on experiments with primates, that quick reconciliation between individuals evolved among social species to preserve important relationships, since group-living organisms that were willing to reconcile with their kin simply had better chances to survive than those who did not, because they were more successful at cooperation.[38]

In a number of studies, Frans De Waal and other researchers have proved this to be true of various kinds of primates.[39] In one of the most conspicuous and quoted experiments by Marina Cords and Sylvie Thurnheer, long-tailed macaques that were taught to cooperate in order to obtain food, experienced a doubling of

---

[37] For the relationship between hierarchy and justice, see Thomas Kazen, "Law and Emotion in Moral Repair: Circumscribing Infringement," *Journal for the Study of the Old Testament* 46.4 (2021): 545–560.

[38] Frans de Waal and van Angeline Roosmalen, "Reconciliation and Consolation Among Chimpanzees," *Behavioral Ecology and Sociobiology* 5 (1979): 55–66; Filippo Aureli and Colleen Schaffner, "Causes, Consequences and Mechanisms of Reconciliation: The Role of Cooperation," in *Cooperation in Primates and Humans: Mechanisms and Evolution* (ed. Peter M. Kappeler and Carel P. van Schaik; Berlin: Springer, 2006) 121–135; David P. Watts, "Conflict Resolution in Chimpanzees and the Valuable-relationships Hypothesis," *International Journal of Primatology* 27.5 (2006); Michael McCullough, *Beyond Revenge: The Evolution of the Forgiveness Instinct* (San Francisco, CA: Jossey-Bass, 2008), 124–127.

[39] For lists of articles, see McCullough, *Beyond Revenge*, 267, or Watts, "Conflict Resolution," 1362.

post-conflict reconciliations.[40] This is not caused by rational consideration, but results from what McCullough calls "the forgiveness instinct,"[41] which is part of the human mind-set, too. Moreover, interpersonal forgiveness in close relationships lowers levels of anxious tension and decreases stress.[42] This means that both forgiveness and revenge are context-sensitive and depend on how we experience our relationship to the perpetrator. Both forgiveness and revenge can give emotional satisfaction. As associations establish forms of fictive kinship and foster close associations, "thick ties," there is an incitement towards forbearance between members which has not only a strong cultural, but also an innate, pull and might counteract the urge for revenge, triggered by competition and hierarchical organisation.[43]

Comparing Rule Texts on Moral Repair

While association texts are numerous,[44] only a few of them present rules relating to moral infringements and moral repair. The texts relevant to our discussion have all been on the table before and the most important have already previously been used in comparative research.

The rule texts from Qumran, including the Damascus document, are thoroughly researched. There are several examples of disciplinary measures to be found within these texts, although they deal with a pretty limited range of infringements, mainly violations of the community counsel, acts which endanger trust, and disturbances of community meetings and community purity, as Jutta Jokiranta points out in the summary of her analysis.[45]

Synagogue studies have flourished during the last decades, but synagogue inscriptions, whether on stone or in mosaic, are mostly late and almost never refer to disciplinary measures, which would be relevant for a discussion of moral infringements and moral repair. This also seems to apply to rabbinic evidence concerning

---

[40] Marina Cords and Sylvie Thurnheer, "Reconciling with Valuable Partners by Long-tailed Macaques," *Ethology* 93 (1993): 315–325; McCullough, *Beyond Revenge*, 126.

[41] McCullough, *Beyond Revenge*, subtitle.

[42] Ibid., 127–129, with references to research on cardiovascular effects of interpersonal forgiveness, as well as effects on psychological stress.

[43] For fictive kinship in the New Testament, see Timothy J. Murray, *Restricted Generosity in the New Testament* (WUNT 2.480; Tübingen: Mohr Siebeck, 2018), 139–159.

[44] Texts relating to ancient associations number thousands of papyri and inscriptions. Kloppenborg and Ascough, *Greco-Roman Associations* (*GRA* I), vi–vii.

[45] Jutta Jokiranta, *Social Identity and Sectarianism in the Qumran Movement* (STDJ 105; Leiden: Brill, 2013), 106.

the *ḥavurot* in Roman Palestine.[46] The sole exception is the Ein Gedi synagogue inscription, which is usually dated to the late 6th or early 7th century and contains a curse against those who reveal the town's secret.[47]

Pauline texts, on the other hand, attest to a number of inter-human and intra-group social conflict areas, which can be profitably compared to disciplinary association rules, even though the latter mostly limit themselves to issues of proper behaviour in the meetings and observing the hierarchical order between members at the banquets. Other texts, too, notably from the gospel of Matthew, present suggestions for how to handle inter-group conflicts in association-like manners.

In the following, I will not discuss norm infringements in general, but focus on interpersonal conflicts. I will begin with rule texts found in Qumran and compare these with Greco-Roman rule texts and with early Christian texts. I will in particular look at the Rule for the Session of the Many and the list of regulations (*mishpatim*) and penalties, for judging in examinations of the *yaḥad* (the Penal Code) that we find in 1QS VI, 8b–VII, 25. Then I will discuss the role of reproof and the foregoing of revenge for upholding in-group justice, within the context of a broader Jewish tradition, beginning by comparing rulings from S and D with association texts, and continuing by discussing similar regulations in texts from the early Christ movement, mainly from Paul, but also including some gospel traditions.

Qumran Rule Texts

Two documents from Qumran in particular contain rules for organisation and discipline, somewhat comparable to certain Greco-Roman association texts. These are the *Community Rule* (S) and the *Damascus Document* (D). The *Damascus Document* comes from the Cairo geniza (CD), but fragmentary versions have been found in Qumran, some of which also contain material paralleling the so-called Penal Code in S (1QS VI, 24–VII, 25; e.g., 4Q266 10 and 4Q270 7). The earliest section of S is probably columns V–VII, in some form.[48] The section 1QS

---

[46] Cf. David Instone-Brewer and Philip Harland, "Jewish Associations in Roman Palestine: Evidence from the Mishnah," *Journal of Greco-Roman Judaism and Christianity* 5 (2008): 200–221.

[47] Rachel Hachlili, *Ancient Synagogues—Archaeology and Art: New Discoveries and Current Research* (HdO 1, Ancient Near East 105; Leiden: Brill, 2013), 521–523, lists various interpretations; cf. Weinfeld, *Organizational Pattern*, 58–64, for a comparative discussion.

[48] Sarianna Metso, *The Textual Development of the Qumran Community Rule* (STDJ 21; Leiden: Brill, 1997); Jokiranta, *Social Identity*, 93.

V, 1–VI, 1a is introduced (1QS V, 1) as "the Rule for the men of the *Yaḥad*" (וזה הסרך לאנשי היחד), stating the purpose of the association. After the introduction follows procedures and rules for new members (ואלה תכון דרכיהם על כול החוקים האלה בהאספם ליחד) (1QS V, 7b–VI, 1a), which towards the end of the column turn into general instructions regarding rank in relation to annual inspections and the practice of reproof. A short section (1QS VI, 1b–8a) with general meeting rules[49] bridges over from the previous "rule for the men of the *Yaḥad*" to the subsequent "Rule for the session of the Many" (הזה הסרך למושב הרבים) (1QS VI, 8b–23), of which the latter part (lines 13b–23) deals with initiation. After this follows a section (1QS VI, 24–VII, 25) often called "the Penal Code," introduced as rules for judging at a community inquiry (ואלה המשפטים אשר ישפטו בם במדרש יחד על פי הדברים). This is the part that most frequently has been compared to disciplinary rules and lists of fines in association texts.

The Rule for the Men of the *Yaḥad* (1QS V, 1–VI, 1a) and General Meeting Rules (1QS VI, 1b–8a)

The *serek* for the *ănšê hayyaḥad* in column V describes their separation from the "congregation of evil" and their unity in *torah* and property under the sons of Zadoq (בני צדוק) (1QS V, 1–2). The regulations proper for gathering and initiating new members begin in V, 7. After the repentance and separation of the covenanters has been described and motivated, two special traits of the association, highly relevant to our discussion, are explicated. The first is its markedly hierarchical character (1QS V, 23–24):[50]

23 וכתבם בסרך איש לפני רעהו לפי שכלו ומעשיו להשמע הכול איש לרעהו איש הקטן
לגדול ולהיות

24 פוקדם את רוחם ומעשיהם שנה בשנה להעלות איש לפי שכלו ותום דרכו ולאחרו
כנעוותו

23. They must be enrolled in order, each man before his neighbour according to his understanding and his deeds, for the obedience in everything of a man to his neighbour, of the small to the great, and for 24. their spirits and their deeds to be scrutinised year after

---

[49] The introduction to this part (ב}אלה{ס} יתהלכו) can be read as referring either backwards or forwards; the contents speak about obeying superiors (cf. V, 23) and the role of the priest (cf. VI, 8b). The exact delimitations between the various sections and their relationship to each other are debated issues. Some regard VI, 1b–8a as an interpolation, others argue against this, see Gillihan, *Civic Ideology*, 340.

[50] Hebrew texts are generally quoted from the *Dead Sea Scrolls Electronic Library* (DSSEL), rev. ed. (ed. Emanuel Tov; Leiden: Brill, 2006). Translations, vary, see notes.

year [i.e., annually], for the elevation of a man according to his understanding and per-fection of his path and for his demotion according to his sin.[51]

The hierarchy envisaged here is strict although not static: a member's ranking de-pends on annual examinations of his knowledge and behaviour. The purpose of this is to promote obedience, which is then repeated in the general meeting rules that follow (1QS VI, 1b–8a; perhaps a summarising addition). In 1QS VI, 2 the text states: "The small must obey the great as to work and wealth" (וישמעו הקטן לגדול למלאכה ולממון).[52] With at least ten covenanters present there must be a priest, and "the men shall sit according to rank before him and thus they shall be asked for their counsel in all matters" (ואיש כתכונו ישבו לפניו וכן ישאלו לעצתם לכול דבר) (1QS VI, 4). We must also assume that the hierarchical order applies to the meals then described (1QS VI, 4–5). These issues are laid out in more detail in the subse-quent section.

Hierarchy creates order, but also has its side effects, which the second special trait reveals: competition. Directly after the strict hierarchy has been delineated, the covenanters are instructed about reproof (1QS V, 24b–VI, 1). Competition fuelled by hierarchical ranking, based on knowledge and behaviour, easily leads to slander and vilification. To counteract this, a practice of controlled reproof is out-lined, which is based on Jewish Scripture and tradition, but also has interesting parallels in association texts as well as in the New Testament.[53] I will return to this in a later section.

The Rule for the Session of the Many (1QS VI, 8b–23)

The *serek* for the *môšab harabbim* in VI, 8b–23 assumes the strict hierarchical or-der indicated in the previous sections. First, there is a leadership hierarchy in this section, which Weinfeld understands to consist of the priests (*kohanîm*; 1QS VI, 8), the official at the head of the many (*paqîd*; 1QS VI, 14), and the overseer (*mebaqqēr*; 1QS VI, 12).[54] The interpretation of three offices is not self-evident, however, especially since it is impossible to decide whether line 14 reads *paqîd* or *paqûd*, and since the man appointed as the head of the many in the fragmentary 4Q289 frg 1 a,b 4 seems to be a priest.[55] Moreover, the introduction to this rule

---

[51] My translation.
[52] Or: with regard to property and money, since מלאכה can mean both "work" and "prop-erty," and ממון is both wealth and money.
[53] Cf. Kloppenborg and Ascough, *Greco-Roman Associations* (*GRA* I), 214.
[54] Weinfeld, *Organizational Patterns*, 19.
[55] For a discussion of details, see Gillihan, *Civic Ideology*, 364–365.

mentions three other categories: priests, elders (*zĕqēnîm*) and the rest of the people
(1QS VI, 8–9). But Weinfeld's comparative point is valid, that various guilds and
associations, including early Christ-believers, mention similar lists of named officials, in more or less hierarchical order.[56]

More specifically, the hierarchical order among the members of the *yaḥad* is
conspicuous and in the Rule for the Session of the Many, this is spelled out in
more detail (1QS VI, 8b–13a):

8b   {ה}<ו>זה הסרך למושב הרבים איש בתכונו הכוהנים ישבו לרשונה והזקנים
       בשנית ושאר

9   כול העם ישבו איש בתכונו וכן ישאלו למשפט ולכול עצה ודבר אשר יהיה לרבים
       להשיב איש את מדעו

10   לעצת היחד אל ידבר איש בתוך דברי רעהו טרם יכלה אחיהו לדבר *vacat* וגם אל
       ידבר לפני תכונו הכתוב

11   לפניו האיש הנשאל ידבר בתרו ובמושב הרבים אל ידבר איש כול דבר אשר לוא
       להפצ הרבים וכיא האיש

12   המבקר על הרבים וכול איש אשר יש אתו דבר לדבר לרבים אשר לוא במעמד
       האיש השואל את עצת

13a   היחד ועמד האיש על רגלוהי ואמר יש אתי דבר לדבר לרבים אם יומרו לו ידבר

8b. This is the rule for the session of the general membership, each man being in his
proper place. The priests shall sit in the first row, the elders in the second, then the rest
9. of the people, each in his proper place. In that order they shall be questioned about
any judgement, deliberation or matter that may come before the general membership,
so that each man may state his opinion 10. to the party of the Yahad. None should inter-
rupt the words of his comrade, speaking before his brother finishes what he has to say.
vacat Neither should anyone speak before another of 11. higher rank. Only the man being questioned shall speak in his turn. During the session of the general membership no
man should say anything except by the permission of the general membership, or more
particularly, of the man 12. who is the Overseer of the general membership. If any man
has something to say to the general membership, yet is of a lower rank than whomever
is guiding the deliberations of the party of the 13a. Community, let him stand up. He
should then say, 'I have something to say to the general membership.' If they permit, he
may speak.[57]

All people will sit according to rank, questioning and speaking at the sessions of
the Many should follow the same hierarchical order. Similarly, 1QSa II, 11–22

---

[56] Weinfeld provides examples from the Athenian *Iobakchoi*, Ptolemaic Egypt, and the Pauline letters (*Organizational Patterns*, 19–21).

[57] Transl. Wise, Abegg & Cook (DSSEL 2006).

envisages the *môšab* of the *'anšē hašēm* (the Session of the Men of the Name) as strictly ordered by hierarchy, based on honour and position. The whole structure of 1QSa, with levels of purity and periods of probation, inspires an extended hierarchy, for that matter.

The Penal Code (1QS VI, 24–VII, 25)

The Rule for the Session of the Many outlines a general hierarchical order. After this section follows the so-called Penal Code (the *mišpaṭîm* for judging), a list with detailed descriptions of infringements and stipulated fines. A very similar version followed at the end of at least some versions of the *Damascus Document*, which is attested by a couple of 4Q fragments (4Q266 10 I, 14–II, 15, 4Q269 11 II, 4–II, 2 and 4Q270 7 I, 1–14).[58] In addition, 4Q265 4 II, 2–II, 2 contains a similar list of infringements and punishments.

The infringements addressed in the Penal Code (1QS VI, 24–VII, 25) partly concern disturbances in session, such as interrupting another person, going to sleep in the *môšab harabbîm*, leaving the session without permission (VII, 10–12), and indecent behaviour, such as exposing nakedness, spitting, laughing out loud, gesturing with one's left hand (VII, 12–15). There are penalties for not being loyal, such as lying about property and fraud, including embezzlement of community funds (VI, 24–25; VII, 3–4, 6–8), uttering the name of God (VI, 27–VII, 2), and resisting the truth and teachings of the community (VII, 16–25). Grave breaches of loyalty render expulsion, some of them permanent. But a good part of the details in the Penal Code concern inter-human infringements relating to honour and status, in particular to in-group hierarchy. These include answering a comrade of higher rank with a "stubborn neck" or addressing him snubbingly, rejecting his instruction and rebelling against his authority (VI, 25–27), speaking against the authority of the priests (VII, 2–4), lying, accusing a comrade of sin, including gossiping and behaving in a fraudulent manner against comrades, (VII, 3–6, 15–16). And there is the prohibition against bearing a grudge and taking revenge on one's own (VII, 8–9), relating to the practice of reproof, which will be discussed further below. Most, if not all, of these rules have to do with crucial issues of group dynamics,

---

[58] The relationship between the penal code in Qumran D fragments and in 1QS and the implications that follow is not a part of this examination, nor the classical question of the development of the *Community Rule* and the interrelationship between various versions. For such discussions, see for example Metso, *Textual Development* and Charlotte Hempel, *The Community Rules from Qumran: A Commentary* (TSAJ 183; Tübingen: Mohr Siebeck, 2020).

such as mutual trust, cooperation, and respect for status within a decidedly hierarchical structure.

The Qumran rule texts exemplify most of our theoretical perspectives almost without comment. The structure and organisation make for thick ties. The covenanters and the *yaḥad* in particular can be characterised as *trust networks*, in which people risk their resources by placing them at the disposal of the community, but for the sake of security. In the case of the *yaḥad*, this is taken to an extreme. The cost is a high degree of conformity and submission under a hierarchical system, which nevertheless rewards faithfulness by high rank.

Investments of property, harsh punishments, and fines, as well as strict rules of behaviour, required by the Qumran rule texts, can be viewed as hard-to-fake and *costly signals* of honesty and seriousness, building reputation, and contributing to an individual's advancement in the hierarchy. Although the signals are costly, there is a prospect of delayed benefits in high ranking, but also in religious rewards and divine favour.

Free riders are effectively deterred by fines and punishments. Serious offences and displays of disloyalty may result in permanent expulsion, but for many infringements, including infringements of honour, there is "forgiveness" in the sense of resumed relationships and privileges after a period of punishment or exclusion. The proceedings are in line with what we learn from *game theory* about punishment and resumed cooperation. At the same time, the inherently hierarchical character of the group causes complications. The tension between fairness and dominance, within a context of mutual dependence, creates conflict and competition, which needs to be regulated.

Hierarchy and Seating

Hierarchy was vital to ancient society and so also to Greco-Roman associations, as they organised themselves along the lines of civic society. The Penal Code is often compared to association rules because of similarities in the way sanctions are applied in cases of infringements of etiquette and honour.[59] In most regards, the Penal Code is more elaborate than most of the association rules, even though seating arrangements are not part of this particular section but dealt with in the preceding text. Generally, however, 1QS is more specific regarding internal hierarchy than the association rules we know of.

---

[59] Cf. Weinfeld, *Organizational Pattern*; Gillihan, *Civic Ideology*; Krause, "Qumran Discipline".

The best-known example of an association text, one which has frequently been compared to the *Community Rule*, is the rule of the *Iobakchoi*, a bacchic association in Athens. The text is inscribed on a column that was found on the western slope of the Acropolis and dated to 164/65 CE.[60] The fines meted out for fighting, taking another member's seat, or otherwise abusing another person, suggest an infringement of the hierarchical order as the root problem. This is supported by the context (lines 72b–83):

μάχης δὲ
ἐάν τις ἄρξηται ἢ εὑρεθῇ τις ἀκοσμῶν ἢ
ἐπ' ἀλλοτρίαν κλισίαν ἐρχόμενος ἢ ὑβρί-
ζων ἢ λοιδορῶν τινα, ὁ μὲν λοιδορη-
θεὶς ἢ ὑβρισθεὶς παραστανέτω δύο ἐκ
τῶν Ἰοβάκχων ἐνόρκους, ὅτι ἤκου-
σαν ὑβριζόμενον ἢ λοιδορούμενον,
καὶ ὁ ὑβρίσας ἢ λοιδορήσας ἀποτιν[νύ]-
τω τῷ κοινῷ λεπτοῦ δρ(αχμὰς) κε', ἢ ὁ αἴτιος
γενόμενος τῆς μάχης ἀποτιννύτω
τὰς αὐτὰς δρ(αχμὰς) κε', ἢ μὴ συνίτωσαν ἰς τοὺς
Ἰοβάκχους μέχρις ἂν ἀποδῶσιν.

Now if anyone begins a fight or is disorderly or sits in someone else's seat (*ep' allotrian klisian erchomenos*) or insults (*hybrizōn*) or abuses (*loidorōn*) someone else, the person abused or insulted shall produce two of the *Iobakchoi* as sworn witnesses, (testifying) that they heard the insult or abuse (*hybrizomenon ē loidoroumenon*). The one who committed the insult or the abuse (*ho hybrisas ē loidorēsas*) shall pay to the treasury (*koinon*) twenty-five light drachmae, or the one who was the cause of the fight shall either pay the same twenty-five drachmae or not come to any more meetings of the *Iobakchoi* until he pays.[61]

The language indicates hierarchical seating arrangements and that the infringements concern breaches of honour. The passage continues immediately with details about physical violence (*plēssō*; line 84ff.) and instructions for how the society should administer justice in such cases.

According to an inscription from Lanuvium in Campania, very explicitly dated to the year 136 CE, and regulating worshippers of Diana and Antinous,[62]

---

[60] Kloppenborg and Ascough, *Greco-Roman Associations* (*GRA* I), 241.

[61] Text and translation from Kloppenborg and Ascough *Greco-Roman Associations* (*GRA* I): 243–244, 247.

[62] Date is stated in the inscription's heading. Andreas Bendlin, "Associations, Funerals, Sociality, and Roman Law: The *collegium* of Diana and Antinous in Lanuvium (CIL 14.2112) Reconsidered," in *Aposteldekret und antikes Vereinswesen* (ed. Markus Öhler; WUNT 280; Tübingen: Mohr Siebeck, 2011), 209–296 (210).

"whoever moves from one place to another (*de loco in aḷium locum transierit*) so as to cause turmoil, he shall be fined four sesterces."[63] The text does not explain the situation further, but it seems quite reasonable to assume a similar situation.

Papyrus Michigan V.243 from Tebtunis in the Fayyum (Egypt) contains a rule from an unnamed association, possibly a regulation of a guild of sheep and cattle owners,[64] and is dated to the time of the reign of Tiberius (14–37 CE).[65] It, also stipulates a fine under similar circumstances:

> ὁ δ' ἐν ταῖς εὐωχία⟨ι⟩ς κατὰ κλισίαν προαναπείπτων τοῦ ἑτέρου δότωι περισσότερον τριώβολον τοῦ ἰδίου τόπου ἔκαστος. ἐάν τις τοῦ ἑτέρου κατηγορήσῃ ἢι διαβολὴν ποιήσηται, ζημι(ούσθω) (δραχμὰς) η. ἐάν τις τὸν ἕτερον ὑπονομεύσῃ ἢι οἰκοφθορήσῃ, ζημιο(ύσθω) (δραχμὰς) ξ.

> And each one who in taking seats at the banquets shoves in front of another shall pay an extra three obols for his own place. If anyone prosecutes another or defames him, let him be fined eight drachmas. If anyone intrigues against another or corrupts his home, let him be fined sixty drachmas.[66]

The situation envisaged in this text is similar to that in the *Iobakchoi* rule: at the banquet people might fight about the seats and offend each other, even to the point of prosecution. Whether the rule of the association from Tebtynis assumes a fixed hierarchy among its members is not clear, but the problem definitely seems to be competition for honour.

An earlier text mentioned by Weinfeld[67] as comparative evidence, and also from the Fayyum, is Papyrus London 7.2193 (previously P. Lond. 2710), from the end of the Ptolemaic period.[68] It possibly originates from the Ptolemaic village of Philadelphia and contains the rule of a guild of Zeus Hypsistos. The text reads (lines 13–17):

---

[63] II.25; text and translation in Bendlin, "Associations," 212, 215.

[64] Since members are to pay a fee for cattle as well as for a flock of sheep (P. Mich. V 243 r5): δ, ἀγέλης προβάτων (δραχμὰς) δ, κτηνῶ(ν) (δραχμὴν) α. The translator Arthur Boak thinks it is "barely possible." Elinor M. Husselman, Arthur E. R. Boak, and William F. Edgerton, *Papyri from Tebtunis*. P. 2 (Michigan Papyri 5; Ann Arbor, MI: University of Michigan Press, 1944), 92.

[65] P. Mich. V 243 r1, lines 6b–8.

[66] Transl. Boak. Text and translation Husselman, Boak, and Edgerton, *Papyri from Tebtunis*. P. 2, 96–100. Also available at http://papyri.info/ddbdp/p.mich;5;243.

[67] Weinfeld, *Organizational Pattern*, 28–29.

[68] The reign of Ptolemy Auletes (69–58 BCE) has been suggested. Colin Roberts, Theodore C. Skeat, and Arthur Darby Nock, "The Gild of Zeus Hypsistos," *The Harvard Theological Review* 29.1 (1936): 39–88 (42).

καὶ μ[η]ι̣[δ]ενὶ αὐτῶν ἐξέστωι συντεγματαρχήισεν⁶⁹ μηιδὲ σχίματα⁷⁰ συνίστασ[θαι]
μηιδ᾽ ἀπ[ο]χωρήισε[ιν ἐκ] τῆς τοῦ ἡγ[ου]μένου φράτρας εἰς ἑτέραν φράτραν
καὶ μηδ᾽ ἢ εὐλογ[ήσειν ⁷¹ ἔ]τερος τὸν ἕτερον ἐν τῶι συμποσίωι μηδὲ κακο-
λογ[ήσειν] ἕτερος [τὸν] ἕτερον ἐν τῶι συμποσίωι μηιδὲ λαλήσειν μηιδὲ ἐπ[ικα]λήσειν καὶ μὲ̣ κατηιγορή[σ]ε̣ι̣ν [[α]] τοῦ ἑτέρου …⁷²

It shall not be permissible for any one of them to play the general⁷³ or to make factions
or to leave the brotherhood of the president for another brotherhood, and neither praise
(?)⁷⁴ one another at the banquet or vilify one another at the banquet or to chatter or to
indict or accuse another… (lines 13–17)⁷⁵

Although one of the key words is disputed, the main thrust of this passage is clearly
against factionalism. Also note the juxtaposition of something which again could

---

⁶⁹ Roberts, Skeat, and Nock, "Gild of Zeus Hypsistos," 40 have συντευματαρχήισεν (like
Friedrich Bilabel in *Sammelbuch griechischer Urkunden aus Ägypten*, Bd 5 [ed. Friedrich Preisige,
et al.; Wiesbaden, Harrassowitz, 1955, 130) but left it untranslated (p. 42). Cf. the discussion in
the commentary (1936: 51). https://papyri.info/ddbdp/p.lond;7;2193 (viewed March 10, 2022)
has συνπε ̣ματαρχηισειν. Skeat (*Greek Papyri in the British Museum [Now in the British Li-
brary]*, vol. 7: *The Zenon Archive* [London : Brit. Mus. publ. for the Brit. Libr. board, 1974], 308–
309) discusses Wilcken's suggestion συνπ(ν)ευματαρχήσειν (in the sense of "take the lead in a
conspiration"), but suggests συντεγματαρχήισεν for συνταγματαρχήισεν, with the sense of
"playing the general." Nock originally dismissed this suggestion (Roberts, Skeat, and Nock, "Gild
of Zeus Hypsistos," 51) because he said it "seems impossible palaeographically and is on other
grounds hardly thinkable." It is very hard, however, to find any other alternative which makes
sense and Skeat points out that the rank of συνταγματάρχης is now evidenced. A meaning like
"lead a batallion," "take leadership of a (sub-)group," in the sense of a splinter group, and thus
fitting with the subsequent σχίσματα, would be reasonable, so I follow this line of argument.
⁷⁰ Here all agree that σχίματα must be read as σχίσματα.
⁷¹ Roberts, Skeat, and Nock, "Gild of Zeus Hypsistos," 40) suggest μῆι γ[ε]νεαλογ[ήσειν],
but the exact meaning is unclear. Skeat (*The Zenon Archive*, 308–309) later argued that the ν was
impossible and must be an η. He reluctantly suggests μηδ᾽ ἢ εὐλογήσειν, which I follow here.
This assumes that the author was anticipating μηδ᾽ ἢ … ἢ (neither … nor) but switched to μηδὲ
instead of the second ἢ. https://papyri.info/ddbdp/p.lond;7;2193 (viewed March 10, 2022) suggest the untranslatable γ[̣]νεαγογ[-ca.?-] and thus leaves the reading open.
⁷² Text from Roberts, Skeat and Nock, "Gild of Zeus Hypsistos," 40–41; cf. Bilabel in *Sammelbuch*, vol. 5, 140; but modified by suggestions in Skeat, *The Zenon Archive*, 308–309 (see previous notes). See also https://papyri.info/ddbdp/p.lond;7;2193 (viewed March 10, 2022).
⁷³ For reading συνταγματαρχήσειν, see note 69 above.
⁷⁴ Reading μηδ᾽ ἢ εὐλογήσειν with Skeat, see note 71 above. The meaning remains unclear:
does the prohibition concern panegyric speeches and vilifications alike during the symposium or
should we take εὐλογήσειν as a euphemism for cursing? Since all other items in the list are negative, the meaning might perhaps be that neither cursing, nor vilification is allowed during the
symposium.
⁷⁵ Translation from Roberts, Skeat, and Nock, "Gild of Zeus Hypsistos," 42, but modified
considerably according to suggestions by Skeat, *The Zenon Archive*, 309.

be a matter of seating arrangements according to status (birth) and rules against honour infringements against comrades, both at the symposium. The exact meaning of γενεαλογεῖν in this context is admittedly unclear, if this is indeed the right verb, but the similarity displayed by these three association laws in juxtaposing rules about seating and honour infringements is conspicuous.

Marking status and honour by seating is attested in many contexts. In two subsequent inscriptions from Psenamosis in the Nile Delta from 67 and 64 BCE, because of his generosity a certain Paris "shall have the first couch (at the banquet) for life" (κλισίαν ἔχειν αὐτὸν τὴν πρώτην διὰ βίου).[76] An inscription from the 3rd century CE, found between Kyme and Phokaia, says that Tation, daughter of Straton, paid for the construction of a building and its courtyard (τὸν οἶκον καὶ τὸν περίβολον) and gave this to the Jews, for which the "synagogue of the Jews"[77] honoured her with a golden diadem (χρυσῷ στεφάνῳ) and a seat of honour (προεδρίᾳ).[78]

The importance of seating arrangements for marking status and delineating hierarchies is also attested by certain texts in the New Testament, which at times seem to subvert the general norm.[79] The Markan Jesus criticises the scribes for their wish for status recognition: they want to be greeted in the squares (ἀσπασμοὺς ἐν ταῖς ἀγοραῖς), receive the foremost seats in the synagogues (πρωτοκαθεδρίας ἐν ταῖς συναγωγαῖς), and the best seats at the dining table (πρωτοκλισίας ἐν τοῖς δείπνοις) (Mark 12:38–39).[80] The letter of James (2:1–4) warns the recipients for showing partiality by assigning good seats to rich people (σὺ κάθου ὧδε καλῶς) (Jas 2:3).

The most explicit illustration from the New Testament of how seating arrangements relate to status and honour, comes from Luke 14, where Jesus teaches honour reversal in the context of a banquet and illustrates it with example stories and parables. The Lukan setting is a banquet at the home of a leading Pharisee (14:1) and Jesus observes how the guests compete for the best seats (τὰς πρωτοκλισίας ἐξελέγοντο) (14:7). It is better to choose a lowly seat and be upgraded than to pick a πρωτοκλισία and be shamed (14:8–9). The level of moral infringement in

---

[76] *IDelta* I.446 = *GRA* III.160, lines 12, 27; transl. Kloppenborg, *Greco-Roman Associations* (*GRA* III), 44. Cf. Richard S. Ascough, Philip A. Harland, and John S. Kloppenborg, *Associations in the Greco-Roman World: A Sourcebook* (Waco, TX: Baylor University Press, 2012), 171–172.

[77] Or "Judeans." The συναγωγή here clearly stands for the association of Jews/Judeans, not for the house (οἶκος).

[78] *IJO* II 36 = *GRA* II.106; Harland, *Greco-Roman Associations* (*GRA* II), 95–96.

[79] Jas 2:1–4; Luke 14:7–11; cf. also the criticism Mark 12:39; Matt 23:6; Luke 11:43.

[80] Matthew (23:6) and Luke (20:46) repeat Mark's accusation and Luke uses the material also for constructing a woe against the Pharisees (Luke 11:43).

the Lukan narrative is, however, low compared to the Qumran rule texts and Greek association texts we have looked at. No open conflicts or fights between guests or "members" are portrayed or addressed here, but the importance of hierarchical seating arrangements at meals for marking status and honour is confirmed.

Fines for Fights and Disturbances

Weinfeld has pointed to numerous parallels between the Qumran rule texts and association rules when it comes to attendance and disturbances of order.[81] Besides fines for fighting, striking, and disorderly behaviour in general (see above), the rule of the Iobakchoi prohibits singing, making noise, and handclapping during meetings (lines 63–66). In fact, many rules have fines for general disturbances and also for being absent without cause.[82] Fines are among other things meted out for refusal to help other members, for not taking part at their burials, for various types of abuses and for accusing and prosecuting other members. An inscription found in Liopesi, from the early 2nd century CE, with a rule for *eranistai*,[83] reads: "if someone in the *synod* should cause a fight (μάχην ποιήσῃ), on the following day let him pay a fine (ἀποτινέτω προστείμου), the one who initiated the fight, ten drachmae, and whoever joined in, five drachmae."[84] The cause of the fight is not indicated in this case. Similarly, in one of the Demotic Tebtynis papyri, fines are imposed on people who insult or strike other members, a higher sum for insulting or striking a president or a vice-president, or for doing it repeatedly.[85]

The 1QS Penal Code has many similarities with association rules but is more elaborate than most of them. Gillihan downplays the similarities in view of the fact that the comparisons concern association rules for drinking societies, in which certain disturbances would be expected – yes, people got drunk! The Penal Code on the other hand refers to boring meetings and we should rather look for constitu-

---

[81] Weinfeld, *Organizational Pattern*, 26–30.

[82] For examples of fines for absence, see the inscription from Physkos, *IG* IX/1² 670 = *GRA* I.61 (Kloppenborg and Ascough, *Greco-Roman Associations* [*GRA* I], 292–294), regulating a Dionysic group, and several of the Tebtynis papyri (Ascough, Harland, and Kloppenborg, *Greco-Roman Associations: A Sourcebook*, no. 299, 300, 301, and 302).

[83] Association of moneylenders. Cf. Christian A. Thomsen, "The *Eranistai* of Classical Athens, *Greek, Roman, and Byzantine Studies* 55 (2015): 154–175.

[84] *SEG* 31:122 = *GRA* I.50, lines 5–8; transl. Kloppenborg and Ascough, *Greco-Roman Associations* (*GRA* I), 236.

[85] *PCair-Dem* 30606 = *GRA* III.191 (Kloppenborg, *Greco-Roman Associations* (*GRA* III), 142. Cf. Ascough, Harland, and Kloppenborg, *Greco-Roman Associations: A Sourcebook*, no. 299.

tional analogies.[86] The argument should be considered, even though the reason for brawls and abuse is rarely spelled out in association rules. One of the few instances is the already mentioned P. Mich. V.243, which says: "If a member behaves badly owing to drunkenness (ἐκπαροινήσῃ), he shall be fined whatever the association decides." While the etymological meaning of the verb παροινέω of course is "to misbehave/abuse under the influence of wine," the word can be used more generally for abusing, insulting, maltreating. It is too simplistic to explain all these fines for fights and disturbances as just occasioned by boozing and carousing. They need to be seen within a wider framework of the hierarchical structure of, and competition for honour and status within, voluntary associations. In any case, neither the association rules mentioned so far, nor the Penal Code, restrict themselves to infringements during meals or meetings, even if those are main activities and the groups differ in emphasis.

Gillihan also objects to Weinfeld's comparison of penalties, since the most common penalties in Greco-Roman associations were fines, while in the Penal Code it is normally a reduction of the food ration, which rather resembles Roman military practice.[87] It is true that ration-fines are most common in the Qumran texts, in addition to exclusion from pure meals and, in serious cases, permanent expulsion. But the members of the *yaḥad* did not have their independent economies. Only in the case of embezzlement of community funds is there an issue of monetary compensation and even then there is an option of reduced rations, in case he perpetrator lacks funds to repay the money (1QS VII, 5–8). Gillihan points out that the corresponding penal code in *D* also has ration-fines, although in contrast to members of the *yaḥad*, members of the *Damascus Document* camps were presumably part of monetary economies.[88] In these contexts, the fine seems to be half the ration instead of a quarter,[89] perhaps since members of the camps only ate some of their meals in common, so the ration-fine was more a deprivation of

---

[86] Gillihan, *Civic Ideology*, 407–409.

[87] Gillihan *Civic Ideology*, 390–394. Krause ("Qumran Discipline," 65) thinks this is a better analogy. Food rations, however, play a certain role in some association rules as well since status and honour may be bestowed on people by giving them double portions; cf. *SEG* 31:122 = *GRA* I.50; *SEG* 58:1640 = *GRA* II.149; *IEph* 213 = *GRA* II.128.

[88] Gillihan, *Civic Ideology*, 389–390.

[89] Assuming that the רביעית in 1QS VI, 25 refers to all the punishments/fines (ענש), i.e., reduction of food rations, listed in the following section, which is quite likely, and that the specification of such reductions as "half his bread" (מחצית לחמו) in 4Q265 4 I, lines 5, 8, 10 (whose exact relationship to D is debated), in fact reflects the practice in D "camps."

honour than real food deprivation, while for *yaḥad* members, a ration-fine of one quarter would have had quite serious effects.[90]

There is apparently more to intra-group fights and disturbances than a mere drinking-party would suggest. We have already noticed the tensions created by hierarchical structures: on the one hand order, authority, and obedience, on the other jealousy and competition. Associations of early Christ-believers had their hierarchical structures, too, although they are nowhere specifically outlined, as in association and rule texts; the closest we come are the instructions for supervisors/bishops and servants/deacons in the Pastorals and the implications of the narratives about apostles and deacons in Acts. The Pauline letters attest to rather vague leadership structures. At the same time, informal hierarchies and underlying power structures can often be glimpsed through many of these texts.

The New Testament has nothing like the lists of fines for various types of unacceptable behaviour, which we find in association texts and in the Penal Code. There are traces of conflict, however, to say the least, and the clearest example is probably 1 Corinthians. In 1 Cor 5:11 Paul explains his view on how a sinning "brother" should be treated: by exclusion. "Do not mingle with someone called brother who is a fornicator, a miser, an idolater, an abuser, a drunkard, or a seizer – do not even eat with such a person" (μὴ συναναμίγνυσθαι ἐάν τις ἀδελφὸς ὀνομαζόμενος ἢ πόρνος ἢ πλεονέκτης ἢ εἰδωλολάτρης ἢ λοίδορος ἢ μέθυσος ἢ ἅρπαξ, τῷ τοιούτῳ μηδὲ συνεσθίειν).[91] As others have been pointing out long ago,[92] this can be compared to the punishment of expulsion in the Penal Code. Paul makes clear that his instructions do not concern people in general, but association members and we should assume that the rebuked behaviours are at least in part directed towards other "brothers" – one would expect that those abused or seized ("grabbed"?) were other group members – so that we here have a case of intra-group infringement. Another Pauline text in 1 Thess 4 is suggestive in this regard. After having declared that each one must know how to control his sex organ (v. 4:

---

[90] Krause ("Qumran Discipline," 69–71) emphasises the role of food access for maintaining group boundaries.

[91] Cf. the author of Jude (copied by 2 Peter), who finds it a shame with immoral people feasting with (συνευωχούμενοι) Christ-believers (Jude 12; 2 Pet 2:13).

[92] See for example Heinz-Wolfgang Kuhn, "A Legal Issue in 1 Corinthians 5 and in Qumran," in *Legal Texts and Legal Issues: Proceedings of the Second Meeting of the International Organization for Qumran Studies, Cambridge 1995. Published in Honour of Joseph M. Baumgarten* (ed. Moshe Bernstein, Florentino García Martínez, and John Kampen; STDJ 23; Leiden, Brill, 1997), 489–499; Michael Newton, *The Concept of Purity at Qumran and the Letters of Paul* (SNTSMS 53; Cambridge: Cambridge University Press, 1985), 98–116.

εἰδέναι ἕκαστον ὑμῶν τὸ ἑαυτοῦ σκεῦος κτᾶσθαι), Paul tells his audience not to transgress or exploit a brother "in this matter" (v. 6: τὸ μὴ ὑπερβαίνειν καὶ πλεονεκτεῖν ἐν τῷ πράγματι τὸν ἀδελφὸν αὐτοῦ). Both context and language indicate a situation in which a person, probably of higher status in society, takes sexual advantage of people in subordinate or inferior positions, which is not acceptable within the association, in which members are considered "brothers."

The filial language in relation to moral infringement and repair is also reflected in the Matthean adaptation of the Jesus tradition. In a combination of a saying against showing anger and insulting one's "brother" with a modified Markan saying about prayer and forgiveness (Matt 5:22–24), Matthew creates a rule against intra-group offence and insult, which does not seem to relate to internal hierarchies and relative status. The prohibition against insulting another member parallels association rules, but the markedly hierarchical framework, especially of the Penal Code, is lacking here. The lack of formal hierarchies, however, does not exclude informal ones. The letter of James 3:13–4:3 suggests a situation of envious competition within an association of Christ-believers. Disorder (ἀκαταστασία) comes from jealousness (ζῆλος) and rivalry (ἐριθεία) (Jas 3:16). Conflicts (πόλεμοι) and fights (μάχαι) come from pleasure (ἡδονή). We sense there is more under the surface than just general character formation: competition within an association framework with an informal structure. Traditionally, references to conflict and division in the New Testament letters have often been taken to refer to doctrinal issues (cf. 2 Tim 2:23–24; Titus 3:9). In light of all the examples of status conflicts in association contexts, it is likely that many references to strife and fight have to do with honour and status infringements. "I urge Euodia and I urge Syntyche to come to an agreement, in Christ" (Phil 4:2), i.e., as association members they must not fight and quarrel, at least not on the surface. The *Didache* excludes people who are engaged in a conflict from the meetings, until they reconcile.[93] Competition for influence, status and honour must take place under ordered circumstances.

When we look at Greco-Roman and early Christian association texts through the lens of our theoretical perspectives, similar considerations apply as for the Qumran rule texts. The problems associated with hierarchical structures and arrangements, whether formal or informal, recur constantly. The tension between a

---

[93] *Didache* 14:2: πᾶς δὲ ἔχων τὴν ἀμφιβολίαν μετὰ τοῦ ἑταίρου αὐτοῦ μὴ συνελθέτω ὑμῖν, ἕως οὗ διαλλαγῶσιν, ἵνα μὴ κοινωθῇ ἡ θυσία ὑμῶν. While ἀμφιβολία usually means "doubt" or "ambiguity," it sometimes means fight (cf. Appian, *Civil Wars* 2.11 [77]), and clearly it does here. Cf the concern for the "altar," which is reminiscent of Matt 5:23, although Matthew has no explicit notion of defilement.

community of "equality within a hierarchy" and personal ambitions leads to numerous conflicts. Fees, fines, and punishments function as *costly signals* of loyalty and conformity, keeping internal order in check, besides deterring free riders. The hierarchical social default setting, or the internal hierarchies of a group, do not excuse abuse or overt injustices. Open conflicts need to be curbed. As a *trust network* with thick ties, an association cannot bear too high levels of tension, without damage.

Reproof and Revenge

Group coherence and cooperation is vital for the survival of any social species, especially when living in closely knit and relatively small bands. This makes it necessary to abstain from revenge and to regulate inter-personal conflicts and status infringements by other means, at least within the immediate group. The *valuable relationships hypothesis* sheds interesting light on the intricate balance between the wish for revenge, based on an urge for fairness, and forgiveness and reconciliation, necessary for a functional *trust network*.

In the *Community Rule*, a law of reproof is introduced already towards the end of the Rule for the Men of the *Yaḥad*, and it is closely associated with the strict hierarchy of the group. One of the purposes of ranking according to knowledge and behaviour is said to be to reprove, although one could plausibly argue that the ranking itself contributes to the competitive environment in which a law of reproof is necessary to prevent backbiting. 1QS V, 24–VI, 1 reads:

24b   להוכי^ח

25   איש את רעהו בא[מ]ת וענוה ואהבת חסד לאיש vacat אל ידבר אלוהיהי באף או בתלונה

26   או בעורף [קשה או בקנאת] רוח רשע ואל ישנאהו [בעור]ל[ת] לבבו כיא ביומ{oo} יוכיחנו ולוא

1   ישא עליו עוון וגם אל יביא איש על רעהו דבר לפני הרבים אשר לוא בתוכחת לפני עדים

Each man is to reprove (*hôkiaḥ*) his neighbour (*rēʿēhû*) in truth and humility and in merciful love for a man. *blank* He must not speak to him with wrath or with grumbling or with a hard neck or with a wicked spirit of jealousy and he must not hate him in his uncircumcised heart, but in that day, he must reprove him (*yôkîḥēnû*) and he will not bear his sin upon himself. And also, no man must bring a case against his neighbour (*rēʿēhû*) before the Many, which is not with reproof (*tôkaḥat*) before witnesses.[94]

Since the *yaḥad's* internal hierarchy was based on annual revisions of members' knowledge and behaviour, slander and accusations against fellow members for laxity or disobedience because of jealousy would have been an apparent risk. A practice of reproof is regulated and ritualised: reproof must be performed on the same day as an infringement or insult occurs and no-one is allowed to bring an accusation before the Many without a reproof before witnesses. The wording of the last phrase (וגם ... אשר לוא) makes it possible to understand it either as a further explanation of one single action, or as an additional action, after first having performed reproof before witnesses.

Another apparent risk with jealousy within this strict ranking system would have been animosity and personal revenge. The Penal Code's prohibition against bearing a grudge and taking revenge on one's own (1QS VII, 8b-9a) must be read against this background, too:

8b   ואשר יטו{ס}ר לרעהו אשר לוא {ס}רמשפט ונענש (ששה חודשים) שנה אחת

9a   וכן לנוקם לנפשו כול דבר

And he who bears a grudge (*yiṭṭôr*) against his neighbour (*rēʿēhû*) which is not according to the rule (*mišpat*) is fined (six months) ᵒⁿᵉ ʸᵉᵃʳ. And likewise, for the one taking revenge (*nôqēm*) for himself on account on any matter.[95]

Taking the context and formulations into account, the fine or punishment is supposedly by reduced rations. The prohibition against bearing a grudge (*nāṭar*) and taking revenge (*nāqam*) expands on Lev 19:17–18.

17 לֹא־תִשְׂנָא אֶת־אָחִיךָ בִּלְבָבֶךָ הוֹכֵחַ תּוֹכִיחַ אֶת־עֲמִיתֶךָ וְלֹא־תִשָּׂא עָלָיו חֵטְא׃

18 לֹא־תִקֹּם וְלֹא־תִטֹּר אֶת־בְּנֵי עַמֶּךָ וְאָהַבְתָּ לְרֵעֲךָ כָּמוֹךָ אֲנִי יְהֹוָה׃

You shall not hate your brother (*'āḥîkā*) in your heart. Do reprove (*hôkēaḥ tôkîaḥ*) your associate (*'ămîtekā*), and you will not bear sin because of him. You shall not take revenge (*tiqqōm*) and you shall not bear a grudge (*tiṭṭōr*) against the sons of your people (*bĕnê 'ammekā*), but you shall love your neighbour (*rēʿăkā*) as yourself – I am YHWH.[96]

---

[94] My translation. The last phrase should be understood as "without previous reproof before witnesses."

[95] My translation. The original six months is confirmed by 4Q259, but bracketed with "one year" being added above the line by what is probably a second hand. Hempel, *Community Rules*, 203.

[96] My translation.

This part of the Holiness Code reflects an in-group ethic of non-retaliation and cooperation, aimed at reforming the behaviour of one's companion rather than taking revenge. The point could be that if one does not protest against something wrong, one shares the responsibility, but the context is one of hatred and revenge, so it is perhaps more likely that the point is to reprove instead of retaliating. The *yaḥad* combined this statement with Nahum 1:2, which describes the Lord as taking revenge (*nōqēm*) and holding on to his rage or bearing a grudge (*nōṭēr*). These activities are understood as divine prerogatives and nothing that human beings should effect by or for themselves. Within the community, brothers or companions should instead reprove (hi: *hôkîaḥ*, from *yākaḥ*) each other. This understanding informs the constituting description of the covenanters in CD VI, 20b–VII, 3a, requiring

לאהוב איש את אחיהו 20b

21 כמהו ולהחזיק ביד עני ואביון vacat וגר ולדרוש איש את שלום

1 אחיהו ולא ימעל איש בשאר בשרו להזיר מן הזונות

2 כמשפט להוכיח איש את אחיהו כמצוה ולא לנטור

3a מיום ליום

for each man to love his brother (*'āḥîhû*) like himself; to hold the hand of the poor, the oppressed, *blank* and the resident alien, and for each man to seek the peace of his brother (*'āḥîhû*), and for each man not to violate his own kin and keep away from fornication according to the rule (*mišpat*), for each man to reprove (*hôkîaḥ*) his brother (*'āḥîhû*) according to the command (*miṣwâ*), without bearing a grudge (*nᵉṭôr*) from one day to another.[97]

Their adversaries, on the other hand, are those who behave exactly like this (CD VIII, 5b–6a):

ונקום וניטור 5b

6a איש לאחיו ושנוא איש את רעהו

each man being revengeful (*nāqôm*) and bearing a grudge (*nṭṭôr*) against his brother (*'āḥîw*) and each man hating (*śānô'*) his neighbour (*rē'ēhû*).[98]

---

[97] My translation.
[98] My translation.

The rule is made explicit further on in the *Damascus Scroll* (IX, 2–8a):

2   ואשר אמר לא תקום ולא תטור את בני עמך וכל איש מביאו <מבאי>

3   הברית אשר יביא על רעהו דבר אשר לא בהוכח לפני עדים

4   והביאו בחרון אפו או ספר לזקניו להבזותו נוקם הוא ונוטר

5   *vacat* ואין כתוב כי אם נוקם הוא לצריו ונוטר הוא לאויביו

6   אם החריש לו מיום ליום ובחרון אפו בו דבר בו בדבר מות

7   ענה בו יען אשר לא הקים את מצות אל אשר אמר לו הוכח

8a תוכיח את רעיך ולא תשא עליו חטא

And concerning what [Scripture] says: "You shall not take revenge (*tiqqōm*) and you shall not bear a grudge (*tiṭṭōr*) against the sons of your people (*běnê 'ammekā*)" (Lev 19:18), any man brought into the covenant who brings a case against his neighbour (*rē'ēhû*) which is not in reproof (*hōkēaḥ*) before witnesses and brings it in burning anger or tells it to his elders in order to despise him, he is taking revenge (*nōqēm*) and bearing a grudge (*nōṭēr*). But there is nothing written except: "He takes revenge (*nōqēm*) on his adversaries and he bears a grudge against his enemies" (Nah 1:2). If he kept silent about him from one day to another and then in his burning anger against him spoke against him in a capital case, this testifies against him because he has not upheld God's commandment which says to him: Do reprove (*hōkēaḥ tôkîaḥ*) your neighbour (*rē'ākā*), and you will not bear sin because of him (Lev 19:17).[99]

This understanding informs both D and S and is referred to explicitly in numerous passages.[100] It is clear that the practice of reproof was formalised and ritualised at Qumran, since we have fragments of a record of reproofs, reported to the Overseer in 4Q477.[101] Exactly what this ritual looked like is impossible to know, but we get

---

[99] My translation.

[100] For reproof, in addition to the passages quoted above, see CD VII, 2; IX, 18; XX, 4; XX, 17. Cf. reproving oneself in 1QS X, 11. For bearing a grudge and/or taking revenge, without a full discussion of reproof, in addition to the texts quoted above, see also CD VIII, 5–6, XIII, 18; XIX, 18; 1QS VII, 8–9; X, 20; 4Q266 7 I, 3; and various parallels to CD and 1QS in 4Q fragments.

[101] 4Q477 is a fragmentary list of people rebuked by the Many. Frg. 1 contains remains of three lines of which only one is partly readable: "to let their offences be remembered, and." Frg. 2 contains remains of two columns. Column i only has four extant lines of which three are readable, mentioning "the men of," "their soul and to reprove," and "the camp of the Many on." Column ii has ten lines with at least four mentions of people rebuked, three whose names are extant, all with fragmented motivations. It must have contained a much longer list. Regarding one person, the motivation is that he loves his near kin (אוהב את שיר בשרו). This is usually taken as a reason for him being rebuked, but one may perhaps speculate that the list could also have contained motivations for unaccepted rebukes. Fragment 3 contains one single word: "they rebuked."

a few hints. The problem is, as indicated above, whether the texts describe one action or two. Both Weinfeld and Schiffman separate the reproof itself, a personal confrontation on the same day, from the formal charge before the Many, which must not be brought unless reproof before witnesses for the same behaviour had previously taken place.[102] Gillihan, on the other hand, sees only one act and understands reproof as "from start to finish, a public, formal legal procedure," which "included no private warning at all."[103] In the camps (*D*), reproofs took place before the Overseer (*mebaqqēr*), but in the *Yaḥad* before the Many, which Gillihan thinks met daily and thus could hear charges immediately.[104]

Unpronounced assumptions complicate the case further. Can we really expect general references to reproof, echoing and explicating Lev 19:17, to provide clear pictures of the factual ritual practice? The fragmentary 4Q477,[105] which Charlotte Hempel notices should be called "The Overseer's Record of Rebukes" rather than "The Rebukes by the Overseer," since rebukes were reported to the *mebaqqēr* and not made by him,[106] implies a difference between reproof and bringing an ordinary charge. It is not a court protocol, only a register, and provides no evidence for what elsewhere, both in *D* and *S*, is referred to as "bringing a case."[107] 1QS VI, 1 seems to distinguish bringing a case (וגם...) from same-day reproof, and CD IX, 6 mentions speaking against another in a capital case, which again seems to be something different. Schiffman is probably right that the reproof witnesses are not witnesses to the transgression, but witnesses to the act of reproof.[108] When a capital case was reported to the Overseer, witnesses to the act could have a different role, as is made

---

[102] Weinfeld (*Organizational Pattern*, 38–41, 49) in fact seems to assume a three-step procedure, similar to that in Matt 18:15–17. First a private reproof, then proof with witnesses, and finally bringing the case before the congregation. Schiffman regards reproof as a legal procedure before a case was brought in court, which must be carried in the presence of witnesses, not of the offence but as witnesses to the act of reproof. Schiffman also compares the Qumran practice of reproof with the rabbinic warning (התראה) before an offence (Schiffman, *Sectarian Law*, 89– 109). Weinfeld (*Organizational Patterns*, 75–76) objects to this, as he finds the purpose of התראה different, being an advance warning, while the Qumran reproof is done during or after an offence.

[103] Gillihan, *Civic Ideology*, 222–223.

[104] Ibid., 224–225, 336, 353. One of Gillihan's points is that the covenanters claimed for themselves the same judicial authority as the state.

[105] See Esther Eshel, "4Q477: The Rebukes by the Overseer," *JJS* 45 (1994): 111–122.

[106] Charlotte Hempel, "Who Rebukes in 4Q477?" *Revue de Qumran* 16.4 (1995): 655–656.

[107] אל יביא איש על רעהו דבר לפני הרבים אשר לוא בתוכחת לפני עדים as in 1QS VI, 1 and יביא על רעהו דבר אשר לא בהוכח לפני עדים as in CD IX, 3.

[108] Schiffman, *Sectarian Law*, 94–95; Rikard Roitto, "Reintegrative Shaming and a Prayer Ritual of Reintegration in Matthew 18:15–20," *Svensk Exegetisk Årsbok* 97 (2014): 95–123 (109).

clear from CD IX, 16–22. Here, reproof applies when only one person sees a transgression (IX, 17b–19a):

וידיעהו   17b

18   לעיניו בהוכיח למבקר והמבקר יכתבהו בידו עד עשותו

19a   עוד לפני אחד ושב והודיע למבקר

> ... then he shall make it known to him to his eyes with reproof to the Overseer and the Overseer shall write it by his hand until he does it in the presence of another and he turns and makes it known to the Overseer.[109]

Since the language is partly ambiguous, it is not entirely clear how the reproof to the perpetrator and the report to the Overseer relate to each other. The witnesses mentioned subsequently, are single witnesses to renewed trespasses, after the first reproof and report (IX, 18b–20a). I thus conclude that the act of reproof is separate from bringing a charge and that it was a ritualised personal reprimand in the presence of witnesses, which was then confirmed by the Many and recorded by the Overseer. It is reasonable that the Many would decide whether such a reproof should be recorded or not for future reference. The fragmentary 4Q477 shows that decisions were recorded together with motivations, such as "hot-tempered" or "boastful" or just "bad" (*mērāʿ*; *rōaʿ*). Although only three names are extant, the list must have contained dozens of names and was probably kept as a running ledger. If infringements continued and with renewed accusations, there would eventually be a formal charge.

Many discussions of reproof in Qumran assume halakic trespasses. While such were certainly involved,[110] we should not forget the effects of a strict hierarchical context on envy and competition. The texts talk about jealousy (*qinʾâ*), grudge (*nôṭēr*), and revenge (*nōqēm*). The 4Q477 motivations definitely include interpersonal infringements – one of the culprits is characterised as having short nostrils, i.e., being "hot-tempered" (*qāṣēr ʾappayim*)[111] – and the practising of reproof was explicitly understood to prevent personal revenge.

---

[109] My translation.

[110] James L. Kugel, "On Hidden Hatred and Open Reproach: Early Exegesis of Leviticus 19:17," *Harvard Theological Review* 80.1 (1987): 43–61 (54) points out that the person "need not have offended anyone – he may be guilty of a victimless crime, say, violating the provisions for abstention from work on the Sabbath." This does not, however, explain the frequent references to hatred, envy, and revenge.

[111] 4Q477 2 II, 4.

From *game theory* we learn that in general it is advantageous to resume cooperation ("forgive") relatively soon after an "infringement," rather than resentfully
wait for too long. The Qumran reproof rules can be understood to prevent personal revenge and regulate interpersonal justice in the interests of the larger group.
Jealousy and competition within a hierarchical framework easily create resentment, which damage the group and inhibit trust. The *valuable relationships hypothesis* shows that revenge is dysfunctional in contexts of mutual dependence.
The practice of reproof reduces tension by handing over responsibility for upholding justice to some kind of central agency. To follow the protocol rather than taking personal revenge might also be viewed as a *costly signal*, demonstrating submission and adherence to community norms.

Although a ritual of reproof, as attested in *D* and *S*, may have been particular
to the covenanters and the *yaḥad*, the biblical interpretation they based their practice on was not. It appears more generally in a number of contexts, although in less
judicial and formal ways, as pointed out by James Kugel, who traced the concept
of reproof from Lev 19, through Jesus ben Sira, the Testament of Gad, and the
Qumran rule texts, to Matt 18 and early rabbinic halakic midrashim.[112]

Lev 19 was a popular passage during the Second Temple period. We find it
elaborated on in diverse quarters. When Jesus ben Sira discusses the limits of neigh-
bourly love and the foregoing of revenge (28:1–5), issues of retribution, rebuke,
and bearing a grudge come up, with Lev 19 as a recognisable backdrop.[113]

1 ὁ ἐκδικῶν παρὰ κυρίου εὑρήσει ἐκδίκησιν καὶ τὰς ἁμαρτίας αὐτοῦ διατηρῶν διατηρήσει.
2 ἄφες ἀδίκημα τῷ πλησίον σου καὶ τότε δεηθέντος σου αἱ ἁμαρτίαι σου λυθήσονται
3 ἄνθρωπος ἀνθρώπῳ συντηρεῖ ὀργήν καὶ παρὰ κυρίου ζητεῖ ἴασιν
4 ἐπ᾽ ἄνθρωπον ὅμοιον αὑτῷ οὐκ ἔχει ἔλεος καὶ περὶ τῶν ἁμαρτιῶν αὐτοῦ δεῖται
5 αὐτὸς σὰρξ ὢν διατηρεῖ μῆνιν τίς ἐξιλάσεται τὰς ἁμαρτίας αὐτοῦ

The vengeful (*ho ekdikōn*) will face the Lord's vengeance (*ekdikēsin*), for he keeps a strict
account of their sins. Forgive your neighbour (*plēsion*) the wrong (*adikēma*) he has
done, and then your sins will be pardoned when you pray. Does anyone harbour anger
against another (*syntērei orgēn*), and expect healing from the Lord? If one has no mercy
(*eleos*) toward another like himself, can he then seek pardon for his own sins? If he who
is flesh holds on to anger (*diatērei mēnin*), who will atone (*exilasetai*) for his sins?[114]

Bearing a grudge is here represented by the Greek συντηρεῖ ὀργήν and διατηρεῖ
μῆνιν. Ben Sira also addresses the issue of reproof in 19:13–17, with the Greek verb
ἐλέγχειν, which is similarly used in the LXX of Lev 19.

---

[112] Kugel, "Hidden Hatred"; cf. Roitto, "Reintegrative Shaming," 103–104.
[113] Kugel, "Hidden Hatred."
[114] NRSV with my modifications.

¹³ Ἔλεγξον φίλον μήποτε οὐκ ἐποίησεν καὶ εἴ τι ἐποίησεν μήποτε προσθῇ
¹⁴ Ἔλεγξον τὸν πλησίον μήποτε οὐκ εἶπεν καὶ εἰ εἴρηκεν ἵνα μὴ δευτερώσῃ
¹⁵ Ἔλεγξον φίλον πολλάκις γὰρ γίνεται διαβολὴ καὶ μὴ παντὶ λόγῳ πίστευε
¹⁶ ἔστιν ὀλισθάνων καὶ οὐκ ἀπὸ ψυχῆς καὶ τίς οὐχ ἥμαρτεν ἐν τῇ γλώσσῃ αὐτοῦ
¹⁷ Ἔλεγξον τὸν πλησίον σου πρὶν ἢ ἀπειλῆσαι καὶ δὸς τόπον νόμῳ ὑψίστου

Reprove a friend, lest he did not do it
    and if he did something, so that he may not do it again.
Reprove a neighbour, lest he did not say it and if he said it, so that he may not repeat it.
Reprove a friend, for often it is slander and do not believe every word.
He may slip unwilling and who has not sinned with his tongue?
Reprove your neighbour before you threaten him
    and give room for the law of the Most High.[115]

We see that reproof for Ben Sira has the same double motivation as in Qumran, which originates with Lev 19, namely, to prevent the trespasser from repeating the mistake and to repair interpersonal infringements before they lead to retaliation – the latter based on an understanding of God as having monopoly on revenge (cf. Sir 28:1). Whether Ben Sira envisages any kind of formal ritual proceedings is, however, highly doubtful. This is moral exhortation rather than judicial language.

Kugel also points to the *Testament of Gad*, which warns against hatred towards one's brother, a hatred that will not listen to the words about love for one's neighbour (*T. Gad* 4:1–2; cf. Lev 19:17–18). Hatred wishes to tell everyone if a brother stumbles (ἐὰν γὰρ πταίσῃ ὁ ἀδελφός) and wishes him to be condemned to death (ἵνα κριθῇ περὶ αὐτῆς καὶ κολασθεὶς ἀποθάνῃ) (*T. Gad* 4:3). A practice of reproof is indicated in a subsequent admonition (*T. Gad* 6:3):

ἀγαπᾶτε οὖν ἀλλήλους ἀπὸ καρδίας· καὶ ἐὰν ἁμάρτῃ εἰς σε, εἰπὲ αὐτῷ ἐν εἰρήνῃ, ἐξορίζας τὸν ἰὸν τοῦ μίσους,[116] καὶ ἐν ψυχῇ σου μὴ κρατήσῃς δόλον· καὶ ἐὰν ὁμολογήσας μετανοήσῃ, ἄφες αὐτῷ.[117]

Love one another from heart, and if someone sins against you, talk to him in peace, banishing hate's poison/arrow, and do not hold treachery in your soul. And if he confesses and changes his mind, forgive him.[118]

The motifs from Lev 19 are obvious: love of neighbour and reproof, here represented by speaking peace (εἰπὲ αὐτῷ ἐν εἰρήνῃ), or as in other manuscripts, speaking *in* peace, bearing a grudge (κρατήσῃς δόλον), and forgiveness (ἄφες αὐτῷ). The

---

[115] NRSV with my modifications.
[116] This phrase is lacking from one manuscript tradition (α).
[117] Text from Marinus de Jonge, *The Testament of the Twelve Patriarchs: A Critical Edition of the Greek Text* (Leiden: Brill, 1978) 131–132.
[118] My translation.

admonition to banish the poison of hatred (ἐξορίζας τὸν ἰὸν τοῦ μίσους) approximates the command not to take revenge. Again, this is moral exhortation, but does not indicate any ritualised practice.

This is different from Matt 18:15–17, which seems to envisage a somewhat ritualised practice, as part of a multi-stage process for reproving (ἐλέγχειν) a sinning community member.[119]

> [15]Ἐὰν δὲ ἁμαρτήσῃ [εἰς σὲ] ὁ ἀδελφός σου, ὕπαγε ἔλεγξον αὐτὸν μεταξὺ σοῦ καὶ αὐτοῦ μόνου. ἐάν σου ἀκούσῃ, ἐκέρδησας τὸν ἀδελφόν σου· [16]ἐὰν δὲ μὴ ἀκούσῃ, παράλαβε μετὰ σοῦ ἔτι ἕνα ἢ δύο, ἵνα ἐπὶ στόματος δύο μαρτύρων ἢ τριῶν σταθῇ πᾶν ῥῆμα· [17]ἐὰν δὲ παρακούσῃ αὐτῶν, εἰπὲ τῇ ἐκκλησίᾳ· ἐὰν δὲ καὶ τῆς ἐκκλησίας παρακούσῃ, ἔστω σοι ὥσπερ ὁ ἐθνικὸς καὶ ὁ τελώνης.

> If your brother sins [against you], go and reprove him between you and him only. If he listens to you, you have won your brother. But if he does not listen, take one or two people with you, so that by two or three witnesses every case shall be established. But if he ignores them, tell the congregation. If he also ignores the congregation, he shall be to you like the gentile and the tax collector.[120]

Kugel emphasises that in contrast to the Qumran scenario, here "the reproacher *is* the offended party,"[121] but as I have argued above, this must often have been the context addressed by the Qumran rule texts, too. Matthew here takes a Q saying about warning a brother and forgiving if he repents as his springboard but elaborates on it considerably.[122] While the Q saying reflects the same general tradition or theology of reproof that we find in for example Ben Sira, Matthew indicates a more ritualised practice, although not as formal as in the Qumran rule texts. Dennis Duling suggests that some kind of judicial process lies buried in the Matthean text, as he observes eight conditional sentences in Matt 18:1–5 – a construction typical of casuistic law[123] – and he suggests that the procedure described "masks a group juridical process, that is only the tip of the iceberg."[124] He thinks, however, that Matthew negotiates a reproof practice within a social context characterised by strong group boundaries and limits to offences, with a message of limitless

---

[119] For an in-depth discussion of this passage in the light of the reproof tradition and with a ritual perspective, see Roitto. "Reintegrative Shaming."

[120] My translation.

[121] Kugel, "Hidden Hatred," 55.

[122] Cf. Luke 17:3 (ἐὰν ἁμάρτῃ ὁ ἀδελφός σου ἐπιτίμησον αὐτῷ, καὶ ἐὰν μετανοήσῃ ἄφες αὐτῷ). Note that Luke does not use ἐλέγχω but ἐπιτιμάω and that there are no details about the procedures (private, with witnesses, etc.).

[123] Dennis C. Duling, "Matthew 18:15–17: Conflict, Confrontation, and Conflict Resolution in a 'Fictive Kin' Association," *Biblical Theology Bulletin* 29 (1999): 4–22.

[124] Ibid., 18.

forgiveness and unbounded love within the group, conveyed by the literary context, reflecting Matthew's understanding of Jesus' message and the motivations for reproof in Leviticus.[125]

Rikard Roitto builds on Kugel and Duling, but goes further, claiming that "Matthew 18:15–17 has a decidedly anti-judicial agenda in its interpretation of the Jewish reproof tradition."[126] Roitto suggests that reintegrative shaming is a key issue in Matthew's reproof practice, which effects a return to the norms rather than marginalisation and exclusion.[127] He argues that Matthew "does a subversive reading" of the genre of the penal code.[128] Whether or not this can be proved for the Matthean text, Roitto's observations regarding the efficiency and functionality of the Matthean procedure in terms of reintegrative shaming are certainly plausible. Most importantly, Roitto discusses Matthew's procedure with the help of ritual theory, concluding that the prayer in Matt 18:19 could have been a semi-public ritual of soft reproof, which would have been efficient as "either a crisis ritual that helped the sinner from his dangerous state of sinfulness, or as a binding ritual that retained the sinner in a state of crisis," making community members aware of the offender's status.[129]

Possibly, 1 John 5:16 about the prayer for a sinning brother whose sin is not a sin unto death (ἁμαρτίαν μὴ πρὸς θάνατον; cf. the capital case, the דבר מות, in for example CD IX, 6) could refer to a similar ritual, connected with the reproof tradition.[130] Another text reminiscent of the reproof tradition and suggesting reintegrative shaming is the post-Pauline 2 Thess 3:14–15, which balances between expulsion and correction.[131] A threat of ostracism is declared over those who will not obey the letter: such a person should be pointed out (σημειοῦσθε) and not allowed to mingle (μὴ συναναμίγνυσθαι) with the rest, in order to be shamed (ἵνα ἐντραπῇ), but he should not be considered an enemy (μὴ ὡς ἐχθρὸν ἡγεῖσθε), only admon-

---

[125] Ibid., 18. Cf. the surrounding narratives about the lost sheep and limitless forgiveness (Matt 18:12–14, 21–22). For this view, Duling refers to William D. Davies and Dale C. Allison, *A Critical and Exegetical Commentary on the Gospel according to Saint Matthew*, vol. 2: *Commentary on Matthew 8–18* (Edinburgh: T & T Clark, 1991), 751. One may, however, question whether we are asking for too much of logical and theological consistency from Matthew's decidedly composite text.

[126] Roitto, "Reintegrative Shaming," 98.

[127] Ibid., 98–99.

[128] Ibid., 2015.

[129] Ibid., 118.

[130] Rikard Roitto, "Practices of Confession, Intercession and Forgiveness in 1 John 1.9; 5.16," *New Testament Studies* 58 (2012): 232–253.

[131] Cf. Roitto, "Reintegrative Shaming," 110–111.

ished or rebuked as a brother (ἀλλὰ νουθετεῖτε ὡς ἀδελφόν). This attests to an informal type of reproof, but not fully ritualised.

The general idea of reproving close kin, friends, and neighbours is of course not unique to the early Jewish and Christian contexts reflected in these texts. It is very much in line with Hellenistic notions of reproof. The verb ἐλέγχειν was used not least by philosophers with a range of meanings, from cross-examining, testing, and proving, to refuting, correcting, and shaming. The notion of frank speech (παρρησία), for example in Plutarch, is perhaps even closer to some of the examples of private or semi-private and non-judicial correction mentioned above.[132] But neither in the philosophers, nor in Greek or Roman association rules, do we find formalised and ritualised types of reproof, like the examples from Qumran rule texts and the gospel of Matthew. While there is much in common on a general level, and the latter practices are part of wider cultural developments, formal and ritual practices of reproof for the repair of moral infringements seem to be limited to particular contexts. To what extent the shapes of these practices are influenced by types of ranking and hierarchy is an interesting question. Whether formal or informal, they can nevertheless be understood according to the *valuable relationships hypothesis* as ways to regulate intragroup revenge and avoid its negative effects on group coherence and cooperation.

Intragroup Justice

The reproof tradition is also in accord with a general tendency in voluntary associations to keep conflicts and cases between members away from civic courts. Weinfeld points out that although staying out of court (other than internal jurisdiction) is never explicitly commanded in the Qumran texts, it is assumed, just like in a number of associations. He provides several examples from association texts where this is explicitly stated.[133] According to the rule of the Iobakchoi, the fine is 25 silver denarii for "one who is beaten and does not go to the priest or the *archibakchos* but (instead) brings a charge with the public courts."[134] The previously mentioned regulation of a Demotic cult association from Tebtynis, dated to the middle of the second century BCE, metes out a fine of 50 debens for denigrating

---

[132] Ibid., 103.

[133] Weinfeld, *Organizational Pattern*, 34.

[134] IG II² 1368 = *GRA* I.51, lines 90–94. ἔστω δὲ τὰ αὐτὰ ἐπιτείμια καὶ τῷ δαρέντι καὶ μὴ ἐπεξελθόντι παρὰ τῷ ἱερεῖ ἢ τῷ ἀρχιβάκχῳ, ἀλλὰ δημοσίᾳ ἐνκαλέσαν τι. Kloppenborg and Ascough, *Greco-Roman Associations* (*GRA* I), 244, 247.

another member and 25 debens for bringing a complaint about another member before the authorities, without first bringing a complaint before the association, and 30 debens for taking the matter to court despite an internal ruling.[135] And the previously mentioned Ptolemaic period papyrus from a gild of Zeus Hypsistos prohibits members from indicting or accusing one another.[136]

The tendency to avoid turning to civic courts for intra-group conflicts comes to the surface in some of the Pauline letters, too. In 1 Corinthians, Paul finds the mere idea appalling (1 Cor 6:1–8):

[1] Τολμᾷ τις ὑμῶν πρᾶγμα ἔχων πρὸς τὸν ἕτερον κρίνεσθαι ἐπὶ τῶν ἀδίκων καὶ οὐχὶ ἐπὶ τῶν ἁγίων; [2] ἢ οὐκ οἴδατε ὅτι οἱ ἅγιοι τὸν κόσμον κρινοῦσιν; καὶ εἰ ἐν ὑμῖν κρίνεται ὁ κόσμος, ἀνάξιοί ἐστε κριτηρίων ἐλαχίστων; [3] οὐκ οἴδατε ὅτι ἀγγέλους κρινοῦμεν, μήτι γε βιωτικά; [4] βιωτικὰ μὲν οὖν κριτήρια ἐὰν ἔχητε, τοὺς ἐξουθενημένους ἐν τῇ ἐκκλησίᾳ, τούτους καθίζετε; [5] πρὸς ἐντροπὴν ὑμῖν λέγω. οὕτως οὐκ ἔνι ἐν ὑμῖν οὐδεὶς σοφός, ὃς δυνήσεται διακρῖναι ἀνὰ μέσον τοῦ ἀδελφοῦ αὐτοῦ; [6] ἀλλὰ ἀδελφὸς μετὰ ἀδελφοῦ κρίνεται καὶ τοῦτο ἐπὶ ἀπίστων; [7] Ἤδη μὲν [οὖν] ὅλως ἥττημα ὑμῖν ἐστιν ὅτι κρίματα ἔχετε μεθ᾽ ἑαυτῶν. διὰ τί οὐχὶ μᾶλλον ἀδικεῖσθε; διὰ τί οὐχὶ μᾶλλον ἀποστερεῖσθε; [8] ἀλλὰ ὑμεῖς ἀδικεῖτε καὶ ἀποστερεῖτε, καὶ τοῦτο ἀδελφούς.

How dare anyone of you who has a case against a fellow, process before the unrighteous and not before the saints? Don't you know that the saints shall judge the world? And if the world shall be judged by you, are you then unworthy a court for small disputes? Don't you know that we shall judge angels – what about matters of ordinary life? Then, if you have ordinary disputes, would you appoint as judges people who are nobodies in the congregation? I say this to your shame! Is there really no wise person among you who would be able to judge between his brothers? Instead, brother litigates with brother and does this before unbelievers![137] It is already a complete failure for you to have law-suits among yourselves. Why don't you rather accept injustice? Why don't you rather accept being cheated? Instead, you are unjust and cheat others, your own brothers![138]

We could think of all kinds of interpersonal infringements behind this situation and Eva Ebel points to the fact that the language (ἀδικεῖν, ἀποστερεῖν) suggests business transactions rather than moral vices.[139] The injunction to accept wrongs is faintly reminiscent of Lev 19 and the ideal of non-revenge between "brothers" in

---

[135] *PCair-Dem* 30606 = *GRA* III.191 (Kloppenborg, *Greco-Roman Associations* (*GRA* III: 142), col. 1, lines 17–19. Cf. Ascough, Harland, and Kloppenborg, *Greco-Roman Associations: A Sourcebook*, 181–182 (no. 299).

[136] μηδὲ ἐπ[ικα]λήσειν καὶ μὲ κατηγορή[σ]ειν (*P.Lond.* 7.2193r, lines 16–17). Roberts, Skeat, and Nock ("Gild of Zeus Hypsistos," 53–54) suggest that κατηγορησειν means dragging someone to court, rather than just accusing someone.

[137] I translate this phrase as an exclamation rather than as a question.

[138] My translation.

[139] Ebel, *Attraktivität*, 197.

the sense of neighbours, associates, or compatriots. This connection becomes clearer in Romans 12:17–21: "Do not repay (ἀποδιδόντες) anyone evil for evil ... do not take revenge (ἐκδικοῦντες) for yourselves." Here, as in the Qumran rule texts, a policy of non-retaliation is motivated by God having absolute monopoly on revenge.[140]

Although Matthew 18:15–20 does not explicitly forbid the use of civic courts for intragroup justice, the instructions we discussed in the previous section seem to indicate a similar attitude towards moral repair as we find in Paul. A narrative example is found in Acts 5:1–11, where Ananias and Sapphira are judged by Peter. Even though the narrative cannot be used as evidence for early Christ-associations practising their own jurisdiction, it points in the same direction as the examples from Matthew and Paul. There is no need to make global claims, but a tendency to avoid taking intragroup conflicts to civic courts and a strong incentive to seek and administer justice within the group itself seems to have been characteristic of various kinds of voluntary associations in the ancient world.

From the perspective of the *valuable relationships hypothesis*, it makes sense to solve conflict within the group in order to avoid revenge between group members, which external judicial processes might lead to. Again, submitting to the authority of the group can be seen as a *costly signal*. Seeing all the groups discussed here as *trust networks*, we can also understand the reticence against turning to external authorities for adjudication from a markedly social perspective. As a *trust network*, an association must maintain its thick ties and guard its advantage in comparison with other social networks, including cities and states, with regard to risk, investment, confidence, and protection. As a *trust network*, an association stands by default in a certain tension with the authorities, even when relations are benign. From such a perspective, the insistence on intra-group judicial authority is only natural.

Comparisons and Conclusions

We have studied and compared rule texts from Qumran, from some Greco-Roman associations, and a selection of relevant early Christian texts. The focus has been on retribution and repair of interpersonal infringements in these associa-

---

[140] The discussion of revenge in Paul and in particular of the expression "heap glowing coals upon his head" is extensive; for one fairly recent example, see John W. Martens, "Burning Questions in Romans 12:20: What Is the Meaning and Purpose of 'Coals of Fire'?" *Catholic Biblical Quarterly* 76.2 (2014): 291–305.

tions, as reflected in the texts. What we find suggests that although these groups were of very different character in many regards, they also shared some common assumptions, common norms, and common practices. Among these, the ways to regulate and circumscribe members' behaviour through rules, fines, and various disciplinary measures are conspicuous. They all organise a community of neighbours, "brothers," or companions, within various degrees of hierarchical frameworks. They all have to handle the tensions created by ideals of mutuality, sharing, fairness, and equality on the one hand, and basically meritocratic and hierarchical, social structures on the other. Loyal commitment to authorities must be negotiated with individual ambition for status and recognition. They all devised ways to deal with intragroup competition and conflict, in order to avoid interpersonal revenge and defer disciplinary decisions to the association's leadership, without turning to outside authorities.

As we have seen, associations were hierarchical societies. Both the sectarian rule texts and several association rules display a clearly hierarchical order. These hierarchies invite competition and conflict between members, in their attempts to move upwards in the hierarchy. A person's status basically depends on birth and class, but is also affected by knowledge, skill, and behaviour. Honour can be gained or lost. This makes it possible to move in both directions. Hierarchy in a sense then, has to suppress what it evokes and counter the urge for revenge, while inspiring a legitimate striving for status. This requires a volatile balance between inequality and control, which both the sectarian rule texts and some of the voluntary association texts exemplify.

The texts also exemplify interpersonal infringements relating to status and honour, which we should expect to be common problems in small and closely knit groups within a hierarchical framework. In an agonistic society, the need to control personal revenge becomes urgent. This applies particularly to units that are very dependent on a high level of cooperation between its members. Family, kin groups, vocational guilds, and cultic societies all depend on mutual trust and loyalty between members or participants. Although formed to protect mutual interests and gains, such groups are vulnerable.

Gillihan thinks that the covenanters' hierarchy of authority markedly differed from that of Greco-Roman cultic societies[141] and that their social hierarchy finds a closer analogy for example in Xenophon's *Politeia* of the Spartans: even high-ranking officials were eager to subordinate themselves under their superiors and all

---

[141] Gillihan, *Civic Ideology*, 248, discussing *D*.

under the Delphic oracle. In this way, divine authority was reinforced by social hierarchy.[142] Gillihan's point about analogies with civic society is well taken, and the sectarian penal code is clearly more explicit than association rules when it comes to status infringements. But I do not find the underlying understanding of hierarchy markedly different. All assume and exemplify a clearly hierarchical social default structure. And although hierarchy may reinforce divine authority, the immediate social function of the hierarchical structures in question is to strengthen group coherence and shape and reinforce group identity.[143]

The sociocognitive and evolutionary perspectives I have suggested have provided further insights. When viewed as *trust networks*, the tensions between risk and security, conformity to authority and individual ambition, visible in all of these associations, become understandable. The perspective of *trust networks* also makes sense of the way in which these groups institutionalise their own specific norms and distinguish themselves from the rest of society to the extent that they avoid the use of other judicial systems than their own. Their often complicated relationships to authorities is part of these characteristics, and has to do with their thick social relationships and their investment of personal resources into the community.

From the perspective of *costly* or *commitment signalling theory*, we can understand some of the disadvantageous practices and rituals in these associations as basically serving an adaptive function. Membership requirements, high fees, common property, and subordination under a strict code of conduct, can be viewed as such confidence-inspiring *costly signals*. But like donkeys, human beings need not only carrots, but also whips. Punishments and fines, whether in money, food, or fellowship, act as deterrence against free-riding and damage reputation. If you are going to enjoy the benefits of the association, you must also pay the costs and once you are in, the costs for not participating and not following the rules can be quite high. Benefits overbalance the costs when you obey, but costs overbalance benefits when you cheat.

This is also one of the pillars of *game theory*, which sheds light also on some of the detailed regulations. Both sectarian and association rules make distinctions between singular and repeated offences and between trespasses from oversight and by intent. According to *game theory* this makes sense since a single defection may indicate a mistake and an otherwise trustworthy person who behaves transgress-

---

[142] Ibid., 339, discussing 1QS V, 23; cf. 347–348.
[143] See Jokiranta, *Social Identity*, 107–109; cf. Carol A. Newsom, *The Self as Symbolic Space: Constructing Identity and Community at Qumran* (STDJ 52; Leiden: Brill, 2004).

ively may change and become trustworthy again. From such a perspective, rewarding cooperative and conforming behaviour and punishing defection, but taking moderate risks in resuming cooperation and "forgiving" defective behaviour, turns out to be the most profitable strategy.

Intra-group revenge, in the sense of interpersonal revenge within the close community, is highly problematic within such a social species as human beings, dependent as we are on cooperation for survival. The *valuable relationships hypothesis* points out that solutions restricting violence within the group save resources and enhance the fitness of the group. They also improve conditions for the individual, by lowering levels of anxiety and tension.

The avoidance of civic courts and various provisions for solving intragroup conflicts within the association, which is typical of a *trust network*, can be understood as functional from this perspective. Within such relationships, tolerance is higher than in other networks and up to a certain point there is "quick" forgiveness – at least within a limited period of time. Beyond that point, however, there is ostracism. Within the group, conflicts must be kept to a minimum and under control.

The reproof tradition in various early Jewish and Christian contexts can also be understood from the perspective of the *valuable relationships hypothesis*, although within an association, a reproof practice attempts to solve a problem partly triggered by the hierarchical structure of the association itself. The reproof tradition and the rituals it seems to have given rise to is thus a special case, which not only reintegrates or excludes offenders, but also handles the competition that hierarchy inspires, namely the temptation to slander and report rivals for one's own gain.

Acknowledgement: The research for this article was funded by the Swedish Research Council, grant nr. 2016-02319.

Studia Theologica Holmiensia

ISSN: 1401-1557. *ehs.se/sth*

1. Göran Gunner, *När tiden tar slut: Motivförskjutningar i frikyrklig apokalyptisk tolkning av det judiska folket och staten Israel.* 1996.

2. Runar Eldebo, *Den ensamma tron: En studie i Frank Mangs predikan.* 1997.

3. Åke Jonsson, *Skapelseteologi: En studie av teologiska motiv i Gunnar Edmans texter.* 1999.

4. Rune W. Dahlén, *Med bibeln som bekännelse och bekymmer: Bibelsynsfrågan i Svenska Missionsförbundet 1917–1942 med särskild hänsyn till Missionsskolan och samfundsledningen.* 1999.

5. Göran Gunner & Sia Spiliopoulou Åkermark (red.), *Mänskliga rättigheter: Aktuella forskningsfrågor.* 2001.

6. Valborg Lindgärde & Åke Viberg (red.), *Drabbad: Texter om kallelse och helhjärtat engagemang.* 2002.

7. Diana Amnéus & Göran Gunner (red.), *Mänskliga rättigheter: Från forskningens frontlinjer.* 2003.

8. Elena Namli, *Och på en enda kyrka: Ortodox ekumenik i ekumenisk dialog.* 2003.

9. MarieAnne Ekedahl & Björn Wiedel (red.), *Mötet med den splittrade människan: Om själavård i postmodern tid.* 2004.

10. Rune W. Dahlén & Valborg Lindgärde (red.), *En historia berättas: Om missionsförbundare.* 2004.

11. Göran Gunner & Sven Halvardson (red.), *Jag behöver rötter och vingar: Om assyrisk/syriansk identitet i Sverige.* 2005.

12. Göran Gunner & Anders Mellbourn (red.), *Mänskliga rättigheter och samhällets skyldigheter.* 2005.

13.   Sven Halvardson & Göran Gunner, *Vart tar väckelsens folk vägen? En studie av frikyrkligheten i de västvärmländska kommunerna Arvika, Eda och Årjäng.* 2006.

14.   Lars Ingelstam & Johnny Jonsson & Berit Åqvist (red.), *Spår av Gud: En vänbok till Valborg Lindgärde.* 2006.

15.   Hans Andreasson (red.), *Liv och rörelse: Svenska Missionskyrkans historia och identitet.* 2007.

16.   Åke Viberg, *Prophets in Action: An Analysis of Prophetic Symbolic Acts in the Old Testament.* 2007.

17.   Rune W. Dahlén & Runar Eldebo & Owe Kennerberg, *Församling i rörelse: Om församlingsutveckling i västra Värmland.* 2008.

18.   Thomas Kazen, *Issues of Impurity in Early Judaism.* 2010.

19a. Thomas Kazen, *Emotions in Biblical Law: A Cognitive Science Approach.* 2011.

19b. Sven Halvardson, *Kanske alla har rätt – eller fel: Religionsmöten och syn på andra i mångreligiösa miljöer.* 2012.

20.   Kjell-Åke Nordquist (red.), *Gods and Arms: On Religion and Armed Conflict.* 2013.

22.   Josef Forsling, *Composite Artistry in the Book of Numbers: A Study in Biblical Narrative Conventions.* 2013.

23a. Sune Fahlgren, *Vatten är tjockare än blod: En baptistisk kulturhistoria.* 2015.

23b. Ulla Lind, *Kallelse och gärning i Kongokyrkan CEC.* 2015.

24.   Jørgen Thaarup, *Kristendommens Morgenstjerne: Konvergerende teologiske træk med baggrund i østlig tradition hos John Wesley og NFS Grundtvig.* 2015.

25.   Caroline Gustavsson, *Delaktighetens kris: Gudstjänstens pedagogiska utmaning.* 2016.

27.   Rune W. Dahlén & Ulf Hållmarker & Lennart Molin, *Missionsskolan Lidingö.* 2016.

28.   Jørgen Thaarup, *Med venner i lys vi tale: John Wesleys og NFS Grundtvigs konvergerende teologier.* 2016

29.   Hans Andreasson, *Identitet och gestaltning: Väckelseforskning i akademi och kyrka.* 2018.

30. Thomas Kazen, *Smuts, skam, status: Perspektiv på samkönad sexualitet i Bibeln och antiken.* 2018.

31. Sune Fahlgren (red.), *Uppdrag Pastor: Teologi och praktik.* 2019.

32. Sune Fahlgren (red.), *Hela livets kyrka: Pastoral teologi för vigsel, begravning och dop.* 2019.

33. Susanne Wigorts Yngvesson & Charlotte Wells (red.), *Trolösa: Speglingar av Luther i Bergman och Bergman i Luther.* 2021.

34. Thomas Kazen & Susanne Wigorts Yngvesson (red.), *Öppna vyer – lång sikt: Festskrift till Owe Kennerberg.* 2021.

35. Thomas Kazen, *Moral Infringement and Repair in Antiquity.* Supplement 1: *Emotions and Hierarchies.* 2022

36. Rikard Roitto, *Moral Infringement and Repair in Antiquity.* Supplement 2: *Group Dynamics.* 2022.

37. Rikard Roitto, *Moral Infringement and Repair in Antiquity.* Supplement 3: *Forgiveness.* 2022.